Twayne's English Authors Series

Sylvia E. Bowman, *Editor*

INDIANA UNIVERSITY

Denton Welch

(TEAS) 163

DENTON WELCH

DENTON WELCH

By ROBERT PHILLIPS

Twayne Publishers, Inc.   ::   New York

Library of Congress Cataloging in Publication Data

Phillips, Robert S.
    Denton Welch.

    (Twayne's English authors series, TEAS 163)
    Bibliography: p. 177.
    1. Welch, Denton.
PR6045.E517Z8   828'.9'1209   73–16129
ISBN 0–8057–1567–3

To the memory of Lester Grosvenor Wells,
"gentleman and scholar,"
who first introduced me to
the works of Welch

Preface

This study was born of enthusiasm, for I have found Denton Welch's books enjoyable and rewarding ever since I first opened one years ago. I was impressed then by the freshness of his prose, the independence of his spirit, the seeming simplicity of his art. And, after writing this book, I am still impressed.

In the two-and-one-half decades since his death, Welch has been discussed in a number of important surveys of British fiction of the 1940's (as my Checklist shows), but he has not always been criticized intelligently or with any depth or at any length. It is my hope that this book will bring other readers not yet acquainted with Welch, or sufficiently aware of his art, to share my appreciation of his accomplishment. On publication it will be the first critical-analytical book-length study of Welch. At the time I began this study all of his works were out of print as well—a situation which appeared partially rectified by Faber & Faber in England and by the University of Texas in America, who in the late 1960's began jointly reissuing Welch's books in a uniform edition. Whether for financial or other reasons, however, by 1973 only two such titles appeared, and it would appear sales did not justify continuing the series. Hamish Hamilton, in London, recently reprinted two individual titles.

Research libraries seem more willing than publishers to invest in Welch's literary reputation. There already are Welch manuscript and letter collections in The British Museum, in the Berg Collection of the New York Public Library, in Syracuse University, and in the University of Texas. Moreover, critics have compared his work to Jean

Cocteau, Marcel Proust, and André Gide—as well as to Thomas Wolfe, Christopher Isherwood, and Truman Capote! Certainly, at the time of his early death, Welch was achieving recognition as one of the most precocious writers of his generation—a generation which includes Angus Wilson, Nigel Dennis, Lawrence Durrell, William Golding, Iris Murdoch, and Dylan Thomas, all of whom, except Thomas, began publishing their important books some years after Welch was dead. By virtue of living longer and publishing more, his contemporaries have, perhaps, relatively obscured him.

Yet Welch deserves our backward glance for several reasons. He was, first, a writer of highly individual talent working in the tradition of the English picaresque. Moreover, his strong sense of physical and spiritual isolation and his preoccupation with Self produced books which can be seen as belonging within the mainstream of the Existential novel and as precursors of the confessional poetry which have become important literary genres in the last two decades. And, had he written nothing other than *A Voice Through a Cloud*, Denton Welch could command our respect. That book, as Francis Wyndham observes in *The Craft of Letters in England*, is "as likely to survive as anything published since the war." It has already been issued by four separate publishers in four different editions.

The novels, stories, journals, and poems of Denton Welch explore a limited number of symbolic themes which might be read as literal autobiography. But, while he is, certainly, one of the most autobiographical writers to produce a published body of work (as a comparison of the facts in my first chapter and the events in his books reveals), Welch's writing cannot and need not always be interpreted in this manner. It seems to me of greater profit to credit Welch with possessing proper esthetic distance and to consider his works as statements of recurring themes rather than rehashes of biographical details. Welch titled his first book *Maiden Voyage,* and all his books involve metaphoric voyages of one sort or another—from youth to maturity, novitiate to artist, dependence to independence, sickness to health.

Welch's vision, symbology, and concerns seem to lend

themselves particularly to Freudian interpretation, and in a number of instances this approach seemed best to illuminate the work under discussion—especially the overtly and rather outrageously symbolic *In Youth Is Pleasure.* Other works, especially those dealing with Welch's acts of independence and the symbolic conflict of Eastern versus Western cultures, seemed to warrant a Jungian perspective. Recognizing that the unconscious cannot express itself directly because it is a composite of past, present, and future, a timeless alchemy of many dimensions, we have interpreted some of the acts in his books on at least two levels: the one of action, the other of meaning.

For the most part, however, his writings are best seen simply through an unpredisposed (albeit New Critical) close reading of the text. Using a combination of these critical approaches, none of them biographical, my book is intended to carry readers as directly as possible to his creations as such rather than as memoirs. (Excepting, of course, his remarkable *Journals,* which are creative in a special way but which are nonetheless diaries.)

I have, therefore, relegated nearly all biographical information to the opening chapter, which is my attempt at a short but relevant biography. Other than his own *Journals* (which were never published in their entirety) and a few memoirs by his friends—notably Maurice Cranston and Noel Adeney, in her surreptitiously biographical novel, *No Coward Soul*—there has been little printed about Welch's life. It is my hope that this biographical chapter will be a useful contribution toward a life of the writer, should some biographer wish to undertake a fuller account. In any event, the reader should understand certain events in Welch's life to fully comprehend the impetus behind his work. His highly circumscribed and sometimes excremental imagery, for instance, might be partially accounted for by the realization that Welch spent the last thirteen years of his life as a bed-ridden cripple and often in agonizing pain as the result of an automotive accident. Because that chapter is a pioneering venture in Welch biography, I have documented all my sources. The critical chapters which follow it depend less on scholarship than insight; and they also, as a result, pack less baggage in the form of footnotes.

Whenever Welch's reading seems to illuminate his writing, I have made allusion to those books he confessed to having read in his *Journals* and in his private letters. And since Welch believed himself to be a poet, I have included a partial chapter on his accomplishments in that genre, though admittedly his poetry is his least achieved work. Welch also was trained as a painter; but, except for drawing a few parallels and contrasts between his graphic and his literary work, I have felt a consideration of his paintings to be outside the perimeters of this first book-length study of his writings. His paintings may prove to be no more, but no less, enduring than those of that other poet and novelist, E. E. Cummings.

Finally, I have commented only on Welch's published work (though "published" in this sense includes one novel released in a limited edition of 150 copies). While other book manuscripts are available for study by responsible scholars in the British Museum and at the University of Texas, they cannot at this time be considered part of the Welch canon. I have also limited myself primarily to Welch's themes and imagery, though I have included some generic and mythic analysis. While I have included commentary on some of his techniques, structural and specific literary devices will hopefully be subjects for fuller discussion by other critics. Ruby Cohn's essay, cited in the Checklist, is an important beginning.

In undertaking this study I have incurred numerous debts which it is a pleasure to acknowledge in the customary fashion. Foremost I wish to thank the Academic Center Library of the University of Texas, which made copies of its considerable collection of Welch letters and manuscripts available for a longer period of time than either party had anticipated; also the Berg Collection of English and American literature, the New York Public Library, which opened to me its exciting files of the Denton Welch-Peggy Kirkaldy correspondence. Thanks is also due to the former Lena R. Arents Rare Book Room, Syracuse University Library (now the Ernest S. Bird Library), which holds the original manuscript of Welch's "When I Was Thirteen." Thanks is also earned by the Archives of Routledge & Kegan Paul Ltd., which offered use of some Welch letters to his editors at that firm, only later to find most had disappeared since the War.

I am especially indebted to John Lehmann, C.B.E. Other individuals who assisted by volunteering biographical or bibliographical material include, *in England:* Eric Oliver, Welch's literary executor; Richard Ormond, the National Portrait Gallery; Brian Southam, Hector Bolitho, Gerald MacKenzie Leet, the late Sir Herbert Read, and the late Sir Osbert Sitwell; *in America:* Philip Lyman, of the Gotham Book Mart; Mary H. Hirth, Henry W. Wenning, Howard Frisch, E. H. Leoni, Marguerite Cohn, Count Claude Jouglet de Pontavert; the late Lester G. Wells, and the late John D. Gordan. My beloved wife, Judith Bloomingdale, has helped beyond the possibilities of acknowledgement.

Permission to quote from Welch's works has been granted by Eric Oliver; Routledge & Kegan Paul Ltd.; Hamish Hamilton Ltd.; David Higham Associates; Faber & Faber; the University of Texas; and John Lehmann. Poem LIV from Housman's *A Shropshire Lad* is reprinted by permission of Holt, Rinehart & Winston, Inc.; Jonathan Cape Ltd.; and the Society of Authors as the literary representatives of the Estate of A. E. Housman.

Two sections of this book were published originally in *Studies in Short Fiction* and *The Centennial Review.* Thanks is due the editors of those quarterlies for permission to reprint material which appears here, in different form, as Chapters 4 and 5.

The self-portrait by Denton Welch which appears on the dust jacket is reproduced with permission from the Academic Center Library, the University of Texas.

ROBERT PHILLIPS

Katonah, New York

Contents

Chronology

Tonbridge. Met Eric Oliver in November. Exhibited paintings at the Leicester Gallery.

1944 Stories begin to appear in *English Story, Cornhill, Horizon, New Writing;* poems, in *Spectator* and *Life & Letters.* Shares house in the Wrotham district with Eric Oliver. Winter 1944-45, begins writing *A Voice Through a Cloud.*

1945 Second novel, *In Youth Is Pleasure,* published Feb. 22. L. B. Fischer publishes American edition of *Maiden Voyage.*

1946 In March, Welch and Eric Oliver move to "Middle Orchard" in village of Crouch, where he is to spend his last years. American and Swedish editions of *In Youth Is Pleasure* published. *Maiden Voyage* published in Paris.

1947 At the Hopgarden. German edition of *Maiden Voyage.* Writes many short stories.

1948 *Brave and Cruel* published. Works toward completion of *A Voice Through a Cloud.* December 30, dies at age thirty-three.

1950 *A Voice Through a Cloud* published posthumously. Vision Press edition of *In Youth Is Pleasure* (original edition out of print).

1951 *A Last Sheaf* published; edited by Eric Oliver. Readers Union edition of *A Voice Through a Cloud.*

1952 *The Denton Welch Journals,* edited by Jocelyn Brooke, published. Publication of *Discovery: Five Songs for Voice and Piano* by Howard Ferguson, words by Denton Welch (London: Boosey & Co.) Based on the poems "Dreams Melting," "The Freedom of the City," "Babylon," "Jane Allen," and "Discovery," all from *A Last Sheaf.*

1957 Manuscript of *Maiden Voyage* presented to The British Museum (in nine exercise books) by donor Sir Eric Miller.

1958 Publication of *I Left My Grandfather's House: An Account of His First Walking Tour by Denton Welch.* Illustrated by Leslie Jones. Private edition of one hundred fifty copies.

Welch's self-portrait in oils presented to The National Portrait Gallery, London, by a group of six donors, most of them Trustees of the Gallery. The portrait, measuring 18 3/4″ × 15 7/8″, was acquired from James Campbell of the Beauchamp Bookshop, and is now No. 4080 in the permanent collection.

1963 Chapman and Hall issue *Denton Welch: A Selection from His Published Works*, edited by Jocelyn Brooke.

1966 *A Voice Through a Cloud* published in America for first time, University of Texas Press. Reprinted in England by Faber & Faber in hardcover and paperback.

1968 *Maiden Voyage* reprinted by Faber & Faber as second of their uniform edition; consistent in format with the 1966 issue of *A Voice Through a Cloud*.

1970 Edith Sitwell's *Selected Letters, 1919-1964*, published in America, including a number to and about Welch.

1973 Hamish Hamilton reissues both *Maiden Voyage* and *The Denton Welch Journals*.

1974 Present volume, first book-length study of Welch, appears.

In the end one experiences only oneself.
> —Nietzsche, *Thus Spake Zarathustra*

By creating I could recover; by creating I became healthy.
> —Heine

CHAPTER 1

Biographical: The Two Talents and the Pain

I *Prologue*

PITT'S Folly Cottage was a garage in back of a big house near Tonbridge, Kent. The garage was at the end of a long drive and attached to the main house by a covered passage. Beside it was a garden. The cottage proper above the garage was an apartment consisting of just two rooms, a big kitchen and a bathroom. Its most striking feature was a Gothic window from which the inhabitants could survey the surrounding countryside.

The interior of Pitt's Folly Cottage was extraordinary. It was all black and gold, cut glass and Chinese lacquer. Against the end wall, flanking the Gothic window, were two seventeenth-century wooden angels larger than life-size. They and the window dominated the room. There was a bed covered with a velvet spread. Above the bed hung engraved wooden Venetian sconces—a cupid, a huge dragonfly, and a rose. The room's other furnishings included a tiny Dalmetsch harpsichord, an eighteenth-century French chess table with an inlaid marble top, a Louis XVI secretaire, many books and numerous paintings, including an early fifteenth-century Colossus of Rhodes.

If a person were invited to Pitt's Folly Cottage during the 1940's, the host would be upstairs anticipating his guest's arrival, standing at the window between the two angels. As soon as the visitor turned into the drive, he might catch a glimpse of an almost ageless face at that window. At once the face of a boy and a very old man, it registered both childlike joy and unbearable pain. By the time the guest reached the end of the drive, the host was on his way down to meet him. When he emerged into the sunlight, his appearance

was pale and other-worldly. Slight and short, he could himself have been a seventeenth-century angel. He had shy,
bright eyes; his forehead was very high; his throat, very
long; his hair, thick and curly and the color of gingerbread.
When he greeted his guest, the voice was cheerful and free
of affectation.

As the visitor ascended the stairs behind him, if he did
not already know, it would become apparent that his host
was an invalid; he had to adjust his pace to his. By the time
the guest reached the astonishing room overhead, the host
was exhausted from the climb; but he would entertain with
tea and talk of art and writing. He would act as if he were
perfectly well, and his speech would be greatly animated.
He perspired freely when agitated. When the visitor took
leave of him, he would know he had encountered a superior
intelligence and a brave spirit. His name was Denton Welch.
For a brief decade he was one of the remarkable figures in
English letters.[1]

II *Beginnings*

For most creative writers the years of childhood and
adolescence are of singular importance. The events of those
years frequently are the source of, and the key to, all that
is written in adult life. But seldom has the total productivity
of a writer been so shaped by youthful experiences as the
work of Denton Welch. Victim of a tragic accident when he
was only twenty, Welch was an invalid for the rest of his
short life. Frequently unable to walk, largely confined to
one location and familiar surroundings, Welch turned to
writing as a substitute for living. Since events in his adult
life were so limited and so few, his imagination was forever
exploring memories of his active childhood for subject
matter and for solace. Like Alexander Pope, Elizabeth Barrett
Browning, Katherine Mansfield, Marcel Proust, Carson
McCullers, and Flannery O'Connor, Welch was an invalid
who wrote under pain while tilling the private garden of
his imagination. To his books one could apply Proust's sum-
mation of his own *Jean Santeuil*: "It is less than a novel and
perhaps much more, the very essence of my life, gathered
with nothing added to it, in those hours of laceration in which

it was lived. This book was never created; it was harvested."[2] As with Proust, a review of Welch's life is of great importance to the understanding of the implications of his writings.

Maurice Denton Welch was born at six o'clock in the evening of March 29, 1915, in Shanghai. His father was Joseph Welch, an Englishman descended from John Knox; and he was a well-to-do company director with considerable interests in the Far East. His mother, an American, was Rosalind Bassett, a descendant from that branch of the Russell family which had founded New Bedford, Massachusetts; and she had brought to China family heirlooms from five generations.[3] Reared in a convent in Florence, she was a Christian Scientist by faith, and she imparted to Denton an affinity for Mrs. Eddy's teachings which he retained throughout his life. Denton, as he was to be called, was the youngest of three sons. His two brothers, William and Paul, were both sturdy, athletic boys who were to present painful contrasts to the young Denton during his sensitive and sheltered boyhood.

Welch spent much of his childhood in China, but he made frequent trips to England. The first of these was made a year or so after the signing of the World War I Armistice, when he was an infant. From that time until he reached the age of eleven, he traveled with his mother between England —where William and Paul were at school—and China, where his father's business interests remained. In this fashion he traveled completely around the world three times before reaching school age.[4] He spent the summer he was three with his mother and brothers in the Diamond Mountains of Korea; he later wrote that one of his earliest memories was finding bright crystal and amber quartz stones on the Korean soil. He always loved small pretty things, and later collected and surrounded himself with them. In adult life, his eccentric rooms resembled an antique shop.

The spring that he was four Welch went again to England, traveling to Frinton and staying at a house on the port. There his brothers frequently rode ponies while Welch followed behind on foot with his mother. During this period Welch received a fright which he never forgot. His mother missed a lapis lazuli, and the boys' nurse took Paul and Denton with her to report it to the local police. Finding himself in a police station, Welch was terrified: he assumed they were accusing him of stealing and hiding the gem, and he was certain they were going to send him to prison. He created a scene, much to the amazement of the police, and accused his nurse of not properly interrogating him at home before dragging him to jail. He was a very imaginative and emotional four-year-old.

During Christmas of that year Welch was at his grandfather's farm in Sussex, the farm he wrote about in several novels and stories. Welch enjoyed playing in the greenhouse on his grandfather's property; and he, Paul, his mother, and the nurse remained there until late spring. The nurse took him and Paul to his first fair that season, and Welch hated it: he found the spectacle "grotesque and squalid, even the merry-go-round."[5] All his life he detested the commercial and the sensational, as his *Journals* reveal.

After Mrs. Welch had settled William in school, she and Welch spent the summer of his fifth year as guests of friends on a Canadian ranch. In 1921, when six years old, Welch was back in China, living in his parents' comfortable home and attending kindergarten. The grounds of his father's house included a coach house and stables, and his father still maintained an ancient carriage which had belonged to the boys' paternal grandmother. Welch liked going for rides with the family coachman, playing with Paul in the garden, and hiding in the branches of a large camphor tree. But, best of all, he loved playing with his mother's jewels and the stored belongings of his great-grandmother—paraphernalia he played with while his brothers took boxing lessons.

Welch's memoirs reveal that as early as his kindergarten days he felt isolated from his peers, and accounts exist of his being ridiculed for ineptness or superstitiousness. He remained a superstitious person all his life, and one of his short stories is entitled simply "Ghosts." His closest friend recalls that "he had a strong, even a fascinated belief in the existence of ghosts and a hope that one day he might see one."[6] Welch was not entirely joking when, toward the end of his life, he told friends he did not approve of the tradi-

tional drinking at funerals and that if any one touched al-
cohol at his there would be tappings from his coffin![7] On the
other hand, we cannot dismiss as entirely fictional his polemic
against mediums in *A Voice Through a Cloud.* He was, then,
a doubtful believer in the spiritual world.

Welch spent the summer of 1922 in Wei-hai-Wei on Half-
Moon Bay in a house on a cliff, and the young boy passed
many happy hours hunting for beautiful shells with Paul.
A summer of firsts, he saw his first dramatic production, a
Chinese play; and he learned to swim. While Denton Welch
could never be regarded as athletic, there were two physical
activities he came to enjoy very much, hiking and bicycle
riding. His early story, "The Barn," gives us—among other
things—a vivid account of bicycle lessons taken from Paul.
He continued to hike and cycle, even after his accident
which ironically occurred while on bicycle. One of the true
joys of his later life was to ride to a remote spot in the country to picnic alone.

After the 1922 summer idyl, the pattern for the next five
years was soon established: school during the academic year;
travel with his mother in the summer. During this period,
Welch's interest in drawing began to develop. As an adult
he remembered designing dresses for his mother when
he was quite young: "I had that passion for exaggeration
which finally does away with the shoulder-straps and which
splits the skirt almost to the very waist."[8] But his life pattern began to fall apart after several years: something was
wrong with his mother. The boy discerned that she was
very ill, and his impressions of that trauma are recorded in
his fine story, "At Sea." Concerning his fictional counterpart in that tale he relates: "He wanted to sing something so
consummate and wonderful that his mother would turn
over and smile and be happy forever; but he knew that she
was dying and that she could not save herself."[9]

By 1926, his mother was dead. We can only imagine the
profound effect her death had on Welch, who was only eleven
at the time. He had been an adoring and devoted son. Memories of her and their times together crowded his notebooks
and novels for years afterward. Probably in deference to
her memory, rather than through any depth of conviction,

he remained emotionally prejudiced toward Christian Science all his life. There is a touching portrait of Welch being taught hymns by his mother in *In Youth Is Pleasure*. And Jocelyn Brooke relates that, immediately after Welch's horrible accident, it was a Christian Scientist friend of his mother's that he first asked to see.[10] Throughout the books he later wrote we encounter specific and oblique allusions to the Bible, remnants of his early training, such as the elaborate metaphor of Jesus raising the impotent man in *In Youth Is Pleasure* and the near-complete Christian allegory in *Maiden Voyage*.

III *Education*

His mother's death must have made the prospect even more difficult when Welch's turn came to join his brothers and be sent away to school in England. The summer after she died was the one before his matriculation at St. Michael's in Sussex. His father took a house for the summer; and a family friend, a Mrs. Sparks, offered to keep house for Denton and Mr. Welch. Paul was at Oxford. Mrs. Sparks brought her little daughter and her own penchant for meddling; Welch took umbrage at both. He later wrote that Mrs. Sparks did not like him and that he once overheard her telling his father that he should be forced to take boxing lessons the next term at school, a suggestion which made him so furious that he rushed into the room and gave her a verbal lashing.[11] In all probability his dislike of Mrs. Sparks was motivated by unconscious resentment of her performance of certain roles formerly played by his mother.

Very little is known about the academic years in England that follow; for, extensive as Welch's *Journals* are, he did not choose to write much about his experiences in preparatory school. It could be that he had found the separation from home, the loss of his mother, and the regimented schedule of studies and games too distasteful to record. Perhaps in later life he had a "block" against those years. In any case, we are given only the scabrous scenes of Repton in *Maiden Voyage,* the traumatic return to Repton at the conclusion of *In Youth Is Pleasure,* and the one reference to his tenure at St. Michael's when he writes in his *Journals* of his first

tense and unhappy Christmas there.[12] No doubt exists that
he disliked St. Michael's, which was a quite conventional
school, though at the time Welch studied there it provided
special facilities for Christian Scientists.[13] The school was,
doubtless, his mother's choice. Jocelyn Brooke, a school-
mate in a higher form than Welch, has written that it was
a very pure school where "one heard little or none of the
usual schoolboy smut."[14]

While St. Michael's does not figure in Welch's fiction,
it did play an important role in shaping his young psyche.
In a letter to Alex Comfort, (1920-), poet and novelist and
lecturer in physiology, he confessed: "Early adolescence
was, to me, what I can only describe as a *sordid* and fearful time. I was frightened of everything and everything
seemed sullied and 'slimed-over' with this fear. It is really
only just lately (I am now 26) that I have come to realize
what an unpleasant time it was."[15]

In another letter, written during the same year, Welch
tells Basil Jonzen about St. Michael's:

There is a dramatic quality about my memories of it. It is the
religious foundation, of course, and then the complete (in my
case) ignorance of all sex matters: This all mixes up with the death
of my mother. . . .

I am always pressing back into the past remembering these
things and pondering on them. They seem to be only just round
the corner still.[16]

We recall that, as late as 1952, another writer, George Orwell,
was so haunted by his own prep-school days that he wrote
the astoundingly acerbic account ironically titled *Such,
Such Were the Joys*.

One tangible result of Welch's private rumination about
school days was his second novel, *In Youth Is Pleasure;* and
its title is also coolly ironic when taken in this context.
While not specifically "about" either St. Michael's or Repton, the book contrasts the freedom of a boy's holiday interlude with his return to the brute, masculine world of school.
At the novel's conclusion, the schoolboy protagonist is symbolically emasculated by his bigger, stronger classmates.

By the time Welch enrolled at Repton, he was becoming interested in art, architecture, and literature. He developed an adolescent passion for the writings of the English poet Robert Nichols (1893-1944), author of *Ardours and Endurance* and the holder of the Chair of English Literature at the Imperial University of Tokyo. Welch thought Nichols' sonnets better than Shakespeare's. He wrote the poet a fan letter; and, when he received no reply, he nurtured a grudge against Nichols for some time after.[17] Living so much in the mental rather than the physical world, Welch—like another literary Repton alumnus, Christopher Isherwood—found the regime at Repton increasingly distasteful. Finally at age sixteen he ran away from the school. He had no plans for the future, but he could not tolerate the present.

When he escaped to a relative's home, he toured cathedrals along the way; and he derived intense pleasure all his life from visiting empty churches and from absorbing their beauty. The novel *Maiden Voyage* gives us his activities and his frame of mind at this stage of his development. Welch was persuaded to finish the school term, but he would not agree to attend a university. His adjustment problems were given understanding attention by Repton's headmaster, Dr. Geoffrey Francis Fisher (later to become Lord Fisher of Lambeth; or, as he enjoyed being called, The Most Reverend and Right Honorable the Lord Geoffrey Francis Fisher of Lambeth!). Despite Dr. Fisher's persuasions, however, Welch was determined to sever relations with academic life.

He left Repton at term's end and spent an interlude in China, which is dramatized in the last two-thirds of *Maiden Voyage*. During this period he decided to pursue his interests in art; and, when he returned to England in 1932, it was to settle into the more enjoyable role of art student at Goldsmith's College at New Cross. Among his teachers was Edward Bawden, who taught him drawing. Welch was now seventeen, curly-headed and very slight of build. A fellow art student has described her male colleague's appearance this way: "he was like Cherubino or the naughty young man in the Rosenkavalier. His feet were so small that we used to run about in each other's shoes, giggling at everything under the sun." He was, she goes on, like "some diabolical

Lord Fauntleroy," or "Cupid playing with a skull."[18] Once in art school, Welch's taste in clothes ran toward the dandified: he was fond of silk ascots, yellow gloves, and a monocle. He even affected taking snuff. Perhaps he was emulating the legends of Delacroix, who wore delicately tinted lavender gloves, and James McNeill Whistler, who affected an eyeglass.

Welch, who remained at Goldsmith's College for four years, lived with a Christian Scientist landlady, Miss Evelyn Sinclair, at 34 Croom's Hill, Blackheath, in a Queen Anne house which had been altered to accommodate guests. (After he became an invalid, Miss Sinclair left Croom's Hill and became Welch's housekeeper at his several residences.) In the early summer of 1933, after completing his first year of art school, Welch took the first of several long walking tours, this one followed the "Pilgrim's Way" from his grandfather's house at Henfield in Sussex to Canterbury. The posthumously published *I Left My Grandfather's House* is his account of this tour.

The freedom of these summers and the recognition of his talent at school contributed to a new sense of well-being, and he became far more independent and opinionated. He ceased to allow himself to be victimized or bullied, and friends tell many anecdotes of his displays of anger and new-found bravery:

"he was quite oblivious of danger. He simply flew like a cat or a hurt child straight for whatever had offended him. He once told me of a terrible moment in a Kentish lane, when some stupid soldier had tried to hector him in what he considered to be his own country. He hadn't a hope of winning but he flew for him and was knocked unconscious."[19]

Welch gives us a vivid portrait of himself during this period in his fine unfinished novel, published as part of *A Last Sheaf.* In that novel fragment and elsewhere Welch confesses that, while growing in self-reliance, he was not really satisfied with his growth as an artist. He was afflicted with grave doubts about his ability and was unhappy with his progress. Perhaps he expected too much of his student efforts; his later paintings reveal a limited but individualistic vision, a decorative—almost Gothic—world of animals, flowers, seashells, pointed arches, broken pediments, and bovine girls, all executed in infinite detail.

His paintings are, on the other hand, far more feminine in sensibility than any of his writing; their very titles reveal their precious nature: "Cat Patting Bluebells"; "Now I Have Only My Dog"; and "The Animal Doctor Should Put You to Sleep." As a painter, Welch, like James McNeill Whistler, perhaps possessed too much "taste" to be a major artist. What critic Horace Gregory said of Whistler in *The World of James McNeill Whistler* could also be said of Welch: "Even at best, his work is haunted by a shadow of 'good taste' that cloys, that displays the art-collector or the dilettante." In a painting, such a display of excessive taste can be as destructive as none at all; for as Degas remarked to Whistler, "How tiresome it must be to be a butterfly! It's better to be an old bull like me."

In most of his paintings—the girls with animals, the little houses, the still lifes—Welch was ever the butterfly, the lightweight, working under the limitation that he forever was merely making a charming picture. (His last paintings tend to horrify rather than charm, but they remain minor statements.) His drawings are even less ambitious; and, in their crowded composition, they seem as claustrophobic as his existence, fussy and shallow.

Nevertheless, Welch's paintings have charmed a number of critics; and, whenever one surfaces for sale, it commands a good price today in galleries. Welch, however, perceived at an early age the limitation of his achievements in the graphic arts. He was not at all satisfied that he had found his life's vocation when, on June 7, 1935, he left his lodgings and set off by bicycle, dressed like an English schoolboy in a navy blue sweater, to visit his aunt and uncle in the vicarage in Surrey.

IV *Disaster*

On the way, Welch was struck by a woman motorist. The shock and pain are described in unbearable detail in *A Voice Through a Cloud,* his masterpiece describing the spiritual and physical aftermath of the accident. Welch's spine was severely fractured—irreparably so—and there were a great many other internal injuries, including damage to the kidneys. For weeks Welch lay close to death. His condition became exacerbated by tuberculosis of the spine. He lost so much weight that at one point, if we can believe his own account, he weighed less than seventy pounds. He was trundled about from a local hospital, to a small London nursing home, to a Broadstairs sanatorium. In this institution he met a Dr. Easton, the individual called "Dr. Farley" in *A Voice Through a Cloud;* and his friendship with Dr. Easton helped give Denton Welch the courage to survive: "It was as if all the problems and difficulties of the new sick life had been halved, because I had found a doctor who appeared to be human."[20] Their relationship is examined at length in *A Voice Through a Cloud,* one of the most exhaustive doctor-patient relationship portrayals in modern English fiction.

"That obscene accident," as Welch came to call it,[21] radically changed his life. As he wrote in his *Journals,* "Nothing can make up for the fact that my very early youth was so clouded with illness and unhappiness. I feel cheated as if I had never had that fiercely thrilling time when the fears of childhood have left one and no other thing has swamped one. . . ."[22] Sometimes he was literally overcome by thoughts of how radically different his adult life might have been.

After a lengthy partial recovery, Welch was released from the sanatorium and began to lead some semblance of normal life, seeing Dr. Easton when necessary. He was left a cripple, and he had to wear a catheter. His father apparently wanted him to return to London and take a house with him near Adam and Ryder streets, but Welch refused. Instead, he located a flat outside London at Hadlow Road where he and Miss Evelyn Sinclair (his former landlady, and the prototype for the character of "Miss Hellier" in *A Voice Through a Cloud*) moved in February, 1936. On his twenty-first birthday he inherited a sum of money from his mother's estate, which, with his accident settlement and an allowance from his father, allowed him to live without working.

Welch and Miss Sinclair remained in that flat until January, 1940; she did the housework and cooking; he tried to regain his strength and interest in art. He spent long periods in bed; fevers and headaches were common. When able to get about, he walked the countryside and picnicked alone. He loved to sit on river banks and lie in haystacks. And he derived great satisfaction from "finding his food," bringing home containers of mushrooms and berries. His pleasure in procuring food this way was more than mere sport, for his allotments and allowance were such that he was often without funds; and, for this reason, he may have been, in adult life, a vegetarian. His writings are filled with descriptions of his brief foraging and picnicking excursions, and full of exclamations of envy for the healthy and mobile youths he saw working in the nearby fields. He possessed a vicarious need for the strength and youth he had missed. He felt acute guilt at not being able to participate actively in the war effort as well (as he confessed in his poem, "Panacea": "In Total War I lead a life / Epitomized by Chinese Chippendale"), and for a brief time he enrolled in the Air Raid Precaution as a messenger.

Early in 1940, Welch and "Evie" Sinclair moved to "The Hopgarden" at Platt; but their tenure there was brief. Though Welch's infirmities exempted him from going to war, the war came to him in the form of a bomb which damaged the cottage. That destruction, plus the fire that started in the kitchen boiler, forced them to abandon the cottage. After Welch had lived with a family named Gardener on "Pond Farm" for the first six months in 1942, he and Miss Sinclair moved to "Pitt's Folly Cottage," the apartment already described that consisted entirely of a big kitchen and a bath over a garage. He named the cottage after his mother's Boston ancestor, William Pitt Denton. Welch remained there for the next four years.

Despite these disrupting moves, and his frequent confinements to bed, Welch continued to sketch and paint. His letters show that he continually experimented with painting technique and that his friends were always more "painterly" than literary. His paintings were first accepted for public exhibition in 1941 by the Leicester Galleries, London, when he was only twenty-six. He continued exhibiting there for the rest of his short life, as well as at the Leger and Redfern galleries. Once he was thrilled to learn that Dame Rose Macauley, the Bloomsbury novelist (1881-1958), had purchased one of his paintings.

In 1941, Welch did a portrait of Lord Berners and his pet macaw, taken from a photograph in Lord Berners's autobiography, *A Distant Prospect*. (Gerald Hugh Tyrwhitt-Wilson Berners was the fourteenth Baron and also a popular novelist.) Welch titled the portrait "Conversation Piece"; and, when he had completed it, he took it by train to Oxford and engaged a room at the Randolph Hotel. It was one of his very few trips, and he made it because he expected Lord Berners to be sufficiently delighted with the portrait to offer to purchase it. Lord Berners came to the hotel at Welch's request, saw the portrait, and—according to Maurice Cranston's report—complimented Welch on the plumbing in his hotel room! Welch was crushed. Had Berners been more gracious, it would have been one of the few paintings he sold during his lifetime. Welch finally left the painting in the flat of a friend he had known since art school, Helen Roeder, where it hung for many years in the hallway. Lord Berners died in 1950 and the portrait was never bought by his family. How pleased Welch would have been, could he have only known that in 1958 his own self-portrait would be hanging in the permanent collection of the National Portrait Gallery in London! Or that twenty years after his death, the firm of Bertram Rota would be asking one thousand dollars for one of his small, unfinished, unsigned oil paintings.

After the Lord Berners episode, Welch's next painting was a commissioned "romantic portrait" of Alex, the pet pug dog of Lady Morell's daughter, Mrs. Julian Goodman. Welch approached the commission soberly and enthusiastically. That same year one of his paintings was included in the show, "Imaginative Art Since the War," at the Leicester.

When word came of his father's death in China, in November, 1942, Welch was unmoved. His *Journals* reveal his primary emotion was concern whether the death meant cessation of the small monthly allowance his father had been

thereby making Welch Connolly's "discovery." For Welch, the *Horizon* publication was more than fortuitous: the piece was read and admired by both Edith and Osbert Sitwell. When Dame Edith wrote him an effusive letter in which she declared that he was a born writer, her praise was enormously encouraging, because Welch regarded her as the greatest living English writer. This incident began a close literary friendship: Dr. Sitwell took Welch to luncheon at the Sesame Club; they exchanged letters and manuscripts; and she generously offered to write a foreword to *Maiden Voyage* to help properly launch his career. That foreword, published in all editions of the book, concludes: "I feel that Mr. Welch may easily prove to be, not only a born writer, but a very considerable one."

Edith Sitwell was not one to lavish praise on fellow writers and, when she did, it was not without effect. Prior to Welch she had trumpeted Dylan Thomas in the 1930's; her review of his *Twenty-five Poems* was the single most important factor in the establishment of that poet's reputation.[28] In the 1950's, the American novelist James Purdy received her attentions; but it was Denton Welch whom she promoted in the 1940's. Her foreword and her review helped make *Maiden Voyage* one of the most popular books of 1943. It was oversubscribed before publication in May, and the public had to wait several months for a surprised publisher to run a second printing. The novel was chosen as "an additional selection" of the Readers' Union, which sold over six thousand copies alone. The book received enthusiastic reviews as well, and Welch's mail contained admiring letters from Elizabeth Bowen, Edward Sackville-West, and E. M. Forster.[29] Edith Sitwell crowed, "I can't think of a first book that has had a better reception."[30]

No one was more surprised at the book's success than its 28-year-old author. Welch had been warned by Herbert Read that the times very well might be wrong for the appearance of such a subjective novel, with its paucity of politics, ideologies, or concern with the war. Welch himself had written to writer-editor John Lehmann of his fear "that the critics might sneer at *Maiden Voyage* as the story of just one more rather sissified boy who couldn't fit into school life and was bad at games."[31] After the book's enormous success, Welch decided in a moment of uncharacteristic modesty that "the magic of Edith's name must have worked this miracle."[32]

But no matter how strenuously she played fairy godmother, Edith Sitwell could not have won critics like Gerald Hopkins, James Agate, and Elizabeth Bowen to Welch's writing unless it had merit; and *Maiden Voyage* was a remarkably original book. Its reception encouraged Welch to continue writing—though he confessed to Frank Swinnerton that he had no idea what he would write about next.[33] Two months before the official publication of *Maiden Voyage,* Welch began the novel about his 1933 walking tour; but he shortly abandoned it and restricted his writing for some time to daily entries in his journal. The walking-tour book was never finished.

His writer's block, if such it was, did not last long. Welch discovered he was prolific—so long as he wrote remembrances of things past rather than pure fiction. Contrary to the warnings of Dame Edith, he enthusiastically began writing *In Youth Is Pleasure,* another novel about a sensitive young man in an alienated world. For Welch the writing of such books became a catharsis; and, considered together, they formed (in Goethe's well-known phrase) "fragments of a great confession." With a second novel underway, Welch now thought of himself primarily as a writer, and he eventually realized that without his accident he might have become just another painter, or—what he dreaded being most—"a precious young man in a gallery."[34] At times, he felt that his art school education was insufficient for a writer, for he lived in awe of men of letters.

While finishing his second book, Welch wrote a number of short stories. He also resumed writing poetry, which he told Henry Treece he had begun writing when nine years old but had abandoned during prep-school days.[35] Despite the fact that he wrote poetry far longer than prose, he never felt his verse to be very accomplished; and it wasn't. Seen today, his poems are his least impressive literary achievements. Nevertheless, within a short time his poems were being published as readily as his stories and drawings by such periodicals as *Harper's, Vogue, Kingdom Come, The Cornhill, Horizon, New Writing, Spectator,* and *Life and Letters.* He was becoming part of the literary establishment.

In the autumn of 1943, Welch grew a beard and wrote continuously. By January, 1944, the manuscript of *In Youth Is Pleasure* was in the hands of his publisher, who was not pleased. Herbert Read wrote Welch: "I confess to a certain disappointment in that it is a continuation of the theme of your first book and does not yet show your ability to go beyond the autobiographical medium." Read obviously had not comprehended the totality of Welch's subjectiveness—that works largely of the imagination were beyond him.

As the publisher had done with Welch's first manuscript, Routledge had the book thoroughly examined by its attorney, Oswald Hickson, for possible libel and obscenity charges. With *Maiden Voyage,* the company had been especially alarmed by Welch's depiction of private life in English public schools. Herbert Read, who began to regard Welch as literally an enfant terrible, wanted *In Youth Is Pleasure* altered for fear Welch would gain a reputation as a sensationalist.[36] But Welch, who had been approached during 1944 by four different publishers who were interested in his work, was in a position to insist that Routledge publish his second novel as written or not at all. He had consented to certain minor bowdlerizations in *Maiden Voyage,* and he intended to make no concessions with the second book:

I am so tired of all this insistance on ordinariness, dulness, so-called normality (really the most unreal and bizarre thing of all) that I wrote at once to say that I didn't mind being plastered with mud, if *they* didn't mind publishing.

All this makes the book sound terribly scatological and 'naughty' and of course it's nothing of the sort. It's really rather prim, I think; but I suppose I have stressed the hidden fantasy life of the 'hero'. It seems as mild as milk to me, when I think of what goes thro' my head every moment of the day!! It is extraordinary to think of the great wastes of unmentionableness in all our minds. . . .[37]

Routledge relented and published *In Youth Is Pleasure* on February 22, 1945, a year after receiving the manuscript. Again Welch pleased the public and critics alike—and did so without endorsements by Dame Edith Sitwell or anyone else. The novel, which sold out before publication, also went into an immediate second printing; and it was swiftly published in American and Swedish editions. On the home-front it received long and largely positive reviews from most important reviewers, but the American reviews were more cautious. Nevertheless, Welch's reputation as a considerable literary talent was secure in England; and he was asked in October to lecture on "Contemporary Literature" at King's College, Cambridge.

While his public acclaim was a great satisfaction—and a reading of his published *Journals* reveals just how much recognition meant to him—Welch's private life was still difficult. In 1944, he again contemplated suicide. Another time, after convalescence and supposed restoration to normal life, he attempted suicide and burned great quantities of his published manuscripts in despair. He gave his own account of this episode in his sketch, "A Fragment of a Life Story." That was the year of more X-rays and more medical consultations, but there seemed to be nothing anyone could do for his condition. His financial outlook was also bleak since his father's death had eliminated Welch's monthly allowance, as he had feared; and, when his father's will was finally probated, it revealed that he had left everything to his second wife and nothing to Welch.

During these months Welch kept largely to himself; for, although "Evie" Sinclair still hovered in the background to provide domestic care, he did not relish the company of "outsiders." He avoided friendships for fear friends would become regular visitors. "I even feel that people pollute my house who come into it," he wrote early in his *Journals*. And later he stated he would like to erect a roofless tower on top of Gover Hill. Unlike the towers of W. B. Yeats, C. G. Jung, and Robinson Jeffers, Welch's never was built. It was a fantasy based on his desire to retreat from society: "I would like to lie in the tower quietly for ever."[38]

VI   *Friendship*

But Welch was rescued from becoming a recluse by a strong and lasting friendship when in November, 1943, he met a young man named Eric Oliver. Despite differences in background and temperament, the two young men were kindred spirits. Eric also had run away from school at Salisbury when he was only nine, and he had walked for five days from Salisbury to London. As a young boy, Eric had had his picture in a newspaper for rescuing a cat; as a young man, he had won a prize for running. By the time he met Welch, he had held several jobs and was currently a worker for the Kent War Agricultural Executive Committee. Because Oliver felt that his promise was largely unfulfilled, he, like Welch, felt the loss of youth and possibility.

A lively friendship developed. Eric admired Welch's book-knowledge, Welch admired Eric's knowledge of the out-of-doors; and there was much each could teach the other. Welch began visiting him on weekends in Streatham; and in July, 1944—eight months after their meeting—Eric moved into Pitt's Folly Cottage to share Welch's house. He originally came to serve as Welch's secretary, probably to act in similar devoted fashion as did Alan Searle for Somerset Maugham; but he soon became his nurse as well. He also assumed most of the household responsibilities: he sawed the wood, made the fires, did the heavy cleaning. Welch's *Journals* reveal there were many times their personalities clashed; and at others a robust roommate was very much in the way in the tiny apartment full of antiques and cut glass, Chinese screens and seventeenth-century angels. There can be no doubt, nevertheless, that Eric Oliver's friendship greatly helped the lonely writer's difficult last years. Indeed, Welch revised his thinking about the necessity for personal withdrawal:

Surely the terrible mistake is the isolation we place ourselves in, through hate, fear, laziness, greed, pride, stupidity. It leads to nothing but emptiness and the terrible 'left' utterly deserted feeling which inevitably overtakes us when we realize that we have lived and behaved in such a way that not a creature cares whether we're alive or dead.

I have only just begun to see that human relationships are the *only* really important thing on earth. Nothing else means anything without them.

I have so often turned away from them, thinking that it was a good thing to live in isolation; always criticizing, despising, seeing through people, thinking nobody good enough for me. But I know now suddenly what all egoism leads to. It leads to death, negation, nothing. It is as if one were still alive and yet had committed suicide. If one does *no* good, gives *no* happiness, goes out to *no* one, what is the point of living at all?"[39]

Welch became more social. In May, 1945, he spent ten days visiting the house of old friends, Noel and Bernard Adeney, at their home, Middle Orchard in Crouch, which was about ten miles east of his Hadlow cottage; and he also began entertaining more old friends and new literary acquaintances at home. He was a brilliant conversationalist, and he was so strongly intuitive that his guests often accused him of reading their minds. His second brother Paul, who had served in the army in Italy for three years and had won numerous ribbons, visited Welch with their Aunt Dolly in August, 1945.

At all these gatherings Eric kept quietly in the background. During fair weather visitors would encounter Welch sitting on the grass, talking excitedly. Many never realized he sat because he could not walk or that his voice was so frenetic because he was sick with fever. In spite of everything, he was animated as a child; and he laughed and shouted frequently. Eric Oliver has described Welch as "always in a high state of elevation,"[40] and Welch himself often explained his being a teetotaler with the remark, "I am drunk *without* wine all the time, and the wine on top is fatal!" He worked at dispelling the impression he was an invalid: "Unless he was utterly prostrated with a very bad attack, he appeared to be casually resting on his bed, with pillows and cushions carelessly behind him; no comfortable supports, bed tables or writing desks, no washings in bed; when sick, no bowls— the bathroom must be reached"[41] "He would explain a day in bed with some such flippant archaism as 'the vapours', as if he would rather like to be thought of as a hypochondriacal marquise."[42] When Welch was too ill to dress, he greeted guests in a red and violet alderman's robe which he used as a dressing gown. (Indeed, until a week or two before his death, he worked to sustain the illusion he would soon be getting up.)

In July, 1945, Welch bought a car, a small Austin, to help him get about from cottage to the village and back. He enjoyed the red roadster; but, when it had a flat tire, he admitted to Peggy Kirkaldy, his Essex pen-pal (See footnote 43 to Chapter One), his health was such that he abandoned the car on the road until Eric could change the tire for him.[43] When well enough, Welch rode about the countryside, taking in the scenic beauties of the area and visiting interesting old buildings. Whenever a forest was cut or an old church razed, he became upset; and he began writing letters to the Society for the Protection of Ancient Buildings about restoring some of the old local manor houses.

The car was one of Welch's minor luxuries, for these were not easy days financially. He had begun selling some of his antiques for cash. Despite the success of his writing, he claimed to have realized only 238 pounds for two books in England, an American edition, and a Swedish translation. Moreover, the Japanese occupation of Malaya had deprived him of income from his investments there. These were also the wartime days of food rationing. He fared better than some British, however, in that his sister-in-law in Hong Kong, William's wife, kept sending him parcels of food. Other supplements to the pantry came from several of his "fans"—readers in Australia, Canada, and America—who had discerned Welch's fondness for sweets and who sent him tidbits through the mails.[44] These gifts were especially fortuitous since Welch's high temperatures induced his cravings for food.

Welch had begun the novel that was to become *A Voice Through a Cloud* during 1941-42, but he temporarily abandoned that project to write short stories, since many of his stories were being accepted by the better magazines. He had been marketing them himself, but on Edith Sitwell's suggestion he acquired in 1945 the services of her literary agent, David Higham, of Pearn, Pollinger and Higham.[45] His reasons for ceasing work on the novel-in-progress were several: he could realize the artistic and financial rewards of completing a story in a relatively short time, even while writing his customary numerous drafts of each; moreover, novel-length manuscripts were much more fatiguing and took more of his waning strength. Then too, Cyril Connolly had expressed an interest in seeing a collection of Welch's stories, which Hamish Hamilton would publish in book form. During the period, Welch wrote some of his best work, stories such as "The Coffin on the Hill," "When I was Thirteen," "The Trout Stream," "The Fire in the Wood," and "The Hateful Word."

VII *The Last Years*

In the fall of 1945 Welch's health worsened. In addition to his usual maladies, he contracted the flu; and it affected him drastically because of his other weaknesses. He spent weeks in bed, still writing whenever he could. He felt there was not much time left him now, and he resumed work on the unfinished novel *A Voice Through a Cloud.* Then, during the Christmas season, the unexpected developed: his left eye suddenly stopped functioning; the cause was diagnosed as a temporary paralysis of the third nerve, and he had to wear a black eye patch and avoid all eye strain. To amuse himself, he again grew a beard; but he cut it off on the first spring day. "My line is to try to look boyish, not dignified," he told Eric Oliver, a line he also pursued in his writing.

Welch's eye improved; but when his internal maladies worsened, he again became bitter. In April, 1946, he wrote, "I bleed inside; and when it comes out of me, almost fascinating in its disgustingness, I feel full of snarling that I am spoilt. To have always to do every fragment of work with the gloves of sickness sheathing each finger, to have that added! The glove of flesh is thick and deadening enough, without the bewildering adventure of illness never-ending. And if a silly woman in a car ten years ago had driven straight instead of crooked, I should not be whining till I'm stiff all through."[46]

Because of his illness, Welch became increasingly dissatisfied with his lodgings; he felt unduly cramped in the garage apartment, as doubtless he was. Hector Bolitho has described the lack of space that he noticed on his first visit to Welch's apartment:

There was an unfinished portrait on an easel and brushes in a straight line on a table; a pile of books neatly stacked beside the bed, and a small inlaid dining table, all so close together that I could imagine Denton Welch painting, reading, writing, playing the spinet, and eating within the space of a few square yards. Although he could walk in the garden, and work at one of his tasks for a little time each day, he spent most of his time in bed and in the room with too many objects. One absorbed some of the claustrophobia of his life, and the self-analysis such patterns encourage.[47]

But lack of space was not Welch's only complaint. He accused his two landladies (who lived on the estate proper) of regularly eavesdropping on him. Finally, he persuaded his friends, Noel and Bernard Adeney, to make a large apartment for him in their country house, Middle Orchard, at Crouch, near Borough Green in Kent. Welch had long admired the house and had wished to buy it, though it clearly was worth far more than he could afford. More out of sympathy than because of practicality, the Adeneys had their home renovated, leaving only small quarters for themselves. (Mrs. Adeney has treated this transaction at length in her novel based on Welch's life, *No Coward Soul*.) When Welch and Eric Oliver moved to Middle Orchard in March, 1946, it was to be his last residence.

The new arrangement did not suit "Evie" Sinclair, and on May 7, 1946, she left Welch's employ after eleven years. Despite his happiness in achieving residence at Middle Orchard, Welch was not able to enjoy his new digs. His health was rapidly deteriorating, and he spent months in bed. When Edith Sitwell invited him to a large party to be given on September 11, he had to decline because he had not been out of his room for a month. After a brief rally, he spent another month in bed, from November to December 4. In these last years of his life, he came to resemble one of the art objects he would have collected: "His form becoming more angular, he had gained the appearance of an attenuated gothic stone carving, with rugged lines full of stern or impish character. With his regard for personal elegance, he felt to the full the cruel humiliation of the more spectacular attacks of his body, but the almost frivolous disgust which he voiced seemed like a sign of vigour that might overcome the mysterious enemy."[48]

The enemy was not to be overcome. When Dr. Easton visited Welch in early 1947, he could only prescribe certain dietary changes. Welch was plagued with headaches, eye troubles, and high blood pressure; he had no strength to work; he merely lay about, nibbled food, and felt "eaten up with waste." He did manage to produce several paintings, which are reproduced in the posthumous volume, *A Last Sheaf;* and he also drew, when he could, drawings for *Vogue* and other magazines. The Medici Society wrote asking permission to produce a volume of his drawings, but the idea was dropped.

In early 1948 he gathered together the stories he wished to include in the book *Brave and Cruel,* which Hamish Hamilton had agreed to publish. Mostly, Welch continued writing *A Voice Through a Cloud* when he could; for the completion of that novel had become an obsession. He accumulated hand-written chapters through sheer will power, "long after most people in his condition would have adopted the life of a permanent invalid."[49] To the end, Welch never liked to discuss his accident, not even with Eric; and, for this reason, he felt perhaps so compelled to finish this novel about his accident. He could in this way at last exorcize the demon and say what he felt but could never bring himself to verbalize. His accident also helps "explain'" his remarkable productivity. Like prolific Aubrey Beardsley, who was fatally ill with tuberculosis, Welch knew too well that his gifts, were they to find any expression at all, had to be released and find recognition in the shortest possible time.

On August 27, 1948, Welch made what was to be his last public outing, a visit to the celebrated couple Vita Sackville-West and Harold Nicolson at Sissinghurst Castle. Eric drove while Welch, to preserve his strength, lay in back of the car on a tartan rug and two velvet cushions. The visit was not a success, as Welch recorded in his last entry, dated August 31, in the *Journals.* In all probability he was too ill, Miss Sackville-West and Mr. Nicolson too aware of his illness, to promote a rousing good time.

After that engagement, Welch remained in bed at Middle Orchard, and Evie Sinclair returned that autumn to help care for him. He now suffered constant pain that was at times so acute that Eric administered doses of morphia. Nonetheless, Welch pressed forward with the writing of *A Voice Through a Cloud,* a manuscript then, as at the time of his death, untitled.[50] The act of writing induced high temperatures, and after short creative periods he would have to lie immobile and blindfolded. In November, when he developed asthma and could not breathe, he lived in fear that he would choke to death in his sleep.[51] Eric Oliver describes the last weeks of Welch's life:

Towards the end he could only work for three or four minutes at a time and then he would get a raging headache and his eyes would more or less give out. Complication after complication set in, and the left side of his heart started failing. Even then, he made colossal and nearly successful attempts to finish the book. He died on the afternoon of December 30th, 1948, still upheld in his last hours by the high courage which seemed somehow the fruit of his rare intelligence.[52]

The manuscript of *A Voice Through a Cloud,* which was at his bedside when he died, was all but complete. The book of stories, *Brave and Cruel,* appeared in the bookstalls the week his obituaries were published. The eminent poet John Betjeman wrote Welch a letter of complimentary congratulations which was delivered after he had died. The funeral service was held at Wateringbury, in the hop gardens of Kent. About twenty people attended. Welch's remains were cremated in the Charing Crematorium, near Maidstone.

For some time after his death, the fate of *A Voice Through a Cloud* was uncertain. His last publisher, Hamish Hamilton, for some reason was not interested in it. Finally, John Lehmann, who had published some of Welch's stories in his quarterlies and who had his own publishing house, asked to read the manuscript; and he immediately decided to publish it. When the book appeared, Lehmann recalls in his autobiography, the reviews were among the most enthusiastic that his firm had received for any book in its publishing history. Reviewers spoke of "a tragic and unforgettable book," "a work of genius," a "writer born," "a triumph," and of "sunshine blazing through a leaf, showing up every vein." Stephen Spender wrote to Lehmann: "It's one of the most wonderful and terrifying books I've ever read. Certainly the first three-quarters of it make a masterpiece."[53]

Three more books by Denton Welch were published posthumously—*A Last Sheaf*, which contains stories, poems, and paintings; *The Journals*; and *I Left My Grandfather's House*, the walking tour novella. With the other publications, Welch produced a total of seven volumes written during seven pain-riddled years. His death at thirty-three ended an art career as brief as Beardsley's; a literary career as brief as Keats's.

CHAPTER 2

Maiden Voyage

I *Structure and Levels of Meaning*

DENTON Welch's first novel, *Maiden Voyage*, has been thought by many to be no novel at all. Indeed, it is listed in *British Autobiographies Before 1951!*[1] In recent critical surveys both Philip Toynbee and Alan Pryce-Jones also call it an autobiography. And autobiographical it is. The action, which closely follows events in Welch's life, begins at the time he ran away from Repton and ends with his return from China to enroll in art school. In this sense, *Maiden Voyage*, like all Welch's books that were to follow, is part of a continuous but not contiguous autobiography. Denton Welch was a very highly subjective writer, one whose artistic creed was in direct opposition to a Keats or to an Eliot—to name two writers who consciously strove to all but obliterate their own concrete personalities in their writing. Welch specifically aimed at self-portraiture, and his writings constitute an overt display of his personality. The hero of most of his books is even baldly named "Denton Welch," an authorial practice sometimes employed by such disparate writers as Marcel Proust, Somerset Maugham, Norman Mailer, and Christopher Isherwood.

But, because Welch used his own name and the outward events of his life to frame his books, we should not assume that Welch's fictions and poems were simple self-expression —factual reportage of his nights and days. We must recall Sir Herbert Read's admonition that "Selection is also creation." Although most events in Welch's "novels" have their sources in his life, and although a study of his *Journals* and unpublished letters confirms this fact, the use of an event, object, or motif in a work of art is quite different from that in a personal or autobiographical statement. For this reason, the same events recorded in Welch's *Journals* are infinitely more satisfying when recast in his novels. In reading his novels on even the most literal level, Welch's selection of details from his life—their order, arrangement, and embellishment—transforms the raw, experiential details so that they lose specifically personal meaning and begin to become universal human materials,elements of works of art. Moreover, the details he selects often assume outward symbolic value, as we shall see. (In his *Journals* he defined the art of writing as "making each tiny happening into a sign. . . .")

C. P. Snow places Welch as a son of Dorothy Richardson and James Joyce—as one who "set out to write of moment-by-moment experience, the moments of sight, sound, smell, which to such writers seemed the essential stuff of art."[2] While none of Welch's novels is a so-called stream-of-consciousness novel, Sir Charles is correct in isolating Welch's preoccupation with the detail of the moment. In his *Journals*, as well as in his novels, Welch never makes broad generalities or vague statements; every moment has to be dissected into increasingly smaller elements. His method, then, literally is sensational; for, like Thomas Wolfe in *Look Homeward, Angel*, Welch feels compelled to record every sight, sound, smell and feeling.

For Denton Welch, then, all reality is composed of countless shards which we cannot begin fully to realize. But, through focussing upon the bits and pieces—the many half-realized and seemingly unrelated incidents and details—we eventually may come to some understanding of our fate. This vision of reality accounts for the loose structuring of Welch's novels and also explains why *Maiden Voyage* is largely episodic. An open-ended picaresque, the narrative is a parade of small moments followed by small moments, each to be enjoyed while it lasts. This vision also may account for Welch's fondness of the miniature, the delicate, and the antique. The ornate pet graveyard which "Orvil Pym" discovers early in *In Youth Is Pleasure* is, for example, precisely the kind of strange and differentiating detail which absorbed Welch's imagination. As one critic has mused, had Denton

Welch never seen a pet cemetery, he surely would have invented one!

Maiden Voyage is not, therefore, an autobiography, although its events and elements are autobiographical. It is also not exactly a novel as we have come to understand one as "a fictitious prose tale of considerable length, in which characters and actions professing to represent those of real life are portrayed in a plot" (definition courtesy of Webster's *New Collegiate Dictionary*). For Welch's "novels" are neither fictitious, overly concerned with what passes for real life, or deeply plotted; more correctly, they are Romances as that genre was defined by Henry James—books in which one encounters "experience liberated . . . experience disengaged, disembroiled, disencumbered."[3] Events and objects are not so important for what they are as for what they mean. In this sense, Welch's books are "poetic" or "poetic novels" as well as Romances, and the critic-biographer Max Wykes-Joyce rightly compares Welch's reverberating visual sense with that of Gerard Manley Hopkins.

Yet quite obviously, in another sense, the books are "symbolic"—and symbolism, by definition, is a granting to outward things an inner meaning, a practice Welch consistently exercised in his drawings and paintings. It is important to remember that, while Welch made his reputation as a fiction writer, Welch was trained as a painter and believed himself a poet; therefore, his was an education of the senses and emotions through art; and he was also very highly intuitive. By means of imagery and symbols, Denton Welch communicated his day and his night dreams. A book which seems to exist outside of time in the eternal world of childhood, *Maiden Voyage* also evokes the fabulous and the mythical. It is no wonder critic Isabella Athey commented on the "amazing number of levels" of meaning to be found in *Maiden Voyage*;[4] but as we shall see, I submit that there are at least four.

Whether as poetic or symbolic novels, or as Romances, Welch's works must never be interpreted on less than two levels, the level of action and the other of meaning. Sometimes there are, intentionally or intuitively, more than one symbolic meaning, embracing deliberate and unconscious meanings. In the case of *Maiden Voyage,* we have a book which is even more than poetic or symbolic: it is also pre-figurative—or, to use a term currently fashionable, it is "mythic." The world of Welch's imagination can reveal the mythic manner in which all of us reexperience life, the way we live on a variety of levels: thought and action, dream and reality, past and present, appearance and reality, personal and collective. Denton Welch saw, or intuited, how these levels can work together in harmony in a work of art.

Welch's use of myth in *Maiden Voyage,* it must be stated at the outset, was in all probability highly unconscious. He did not consciously employ the "mythical method" of Joyce and Thomas Mann, for nowhere did Welch appropriate a myth or a set of myths and deliberately weave a fictional tapestry about them. In Joyce and Mann, this method is usually successful; in certain recent novels, such as Frederick Buechner's *A Long Day's Dying* and John Updike's *The Centaur,* it is not. Those two novels calculatingly exploit myth and attempt to add depth or counterpoint to the literal, universal implication to the current secular reality through such mythic underpinnings. In both, the literal level and the prefigurative level become incompatible, for the myth and the reality are unsuccessfully interwoven.

On the other hand, Welch was one of those rare mythopoeic artists (like Franz Kafka) whose work unconsciously reflects archetypes from the collective unconscious—a novelist whose work exemplifies not mythology-consciousness (like Updike) but rather a mythic imagination. No better example can be found than *Maiden Voyage,* that poetic novel which successfully operates on a number of levels, the most important of which perhaps is the mythic. As stated earlier, I suggest that *Maiden Voyage* operates on four such levels, two deliberate and two unconscious. The first, or deliberate, level is, of course, the literal. Taken literally, the book is indeed an autobiography of sorts in which the author—by an apparently artless accumulation of details and incidents—makes himself and his problems credible to the reader. On this level, it could be compared with André Gide's *If It Die,* if Welch had not lacked the absolute candor of Gide in sexual matters. On this level, the book needs no explication.

A second deliberate level is that of biblical allegory, for Welch appears to have labored long and hard, during the writing of certain portions of the book, to establish parallels between his book's protagonist and Christ (whom in *Aion* Jung has called "the Western archetype of the Self"). But this religious allegory is not a sustained one; and, like myth in Updike's *The Centaur* or Christian allegory in Faulkner's *Light in August*, it seems inflicted from outside the dream of the book's intention. The very context of the scenes in which the Christian allegory in *Maiden Voyage* is embedded tends to destroy it—an effect which I shall discuss as an afterthought to the chapter.

A third (and unconscious) level is the symbolic, or metaphoric, in which Welch's trip to China becomes his journey toward self-realization. In this context, the book is another Romance of rites of passage, such as Charles Dickens's *Great Expectations*, D. H. Lawrence's *Sons and Lovers*, or Somerset Maugham's *Of Human Bondage*. Thus the "maiden voyage" of the title is Welch's first journey into the world of experience, and he is maiden (virgin) in regard to worldly knowledge. This interpretation should be examined first, since *Maiden Voyage* is alive with metaphorical suggestions. Such an examination of the symbols and actions within this novel should be at greater depth than that of any of his other books, in order for us to comprehend at the outset how dense the textures of Welch's books really are. Very often what seems charming and spontaneous writing reveals itself to be a carefully woven tapestry of literary intentions.

Finally, there is a second unconscious level, that of mythological allegory. Here Welch has written an archetypal romance based almost literally on the ubiquitous monomyth of the Hero's Adventure. This rich mythic meaning no critic has yet explored, which is perhaps the most rewarding reason for reexamining *Maiden Voyage* some thirty years after its publication.

II *Symbols and Metaphors*

"After I had run away from school, no one knew what to do with me. I sat in my cousin's London drawing-room, listening to my relations as they talked. I did not know what was going to happen to me."[5] *Maiden Voyage* begins with Welch immediately conveying the hero's sense of isolation, his spiritual dissociation from those around him. The protagonist finds himself between two worlds, belonging to neither. Young Denton (as the hero is named) has elected to separate himself from his contemporaries at school; yet he is not a part of the adult world to which he has fled. He has even been rejected by the world between the two extremes, that of adolescence; for his brother and his teenage friends ridicule him and do not think him manly enough. Consequently, Denton is possessed by a terrible sense of inadequacy, one that is exacerbated by his delicate physical nature which puts him at a disadvantage in the school's rigorous fag system. Yet running away from Repton has solved nothing; for, once in the world, physical inadequacy is displaced by occupational inadequacy. He wishes he could hold an ordinary job like an ordinary person, "But I felt that I was not good for anything"(8).

Paradoxically, Denton feels the pull of a vocational calling. During his five days' lark away from school he already has set the pattern for his future life; for, instead of playing or working or drinking, he has visited cathedrals. The pull toward art, solitude, and religion has been felt. He is rebelling against the life and education of the upperclasses; and, as in Evelyn Waugh's first novel, *Decline and Fall,* Welch's first book gives us a portrait of dissipation among the well-to-do in which the public school serves as a microcosm of the greater society.

The title of the novel is significant. This truancy marks Denton's first trip alone, and the account of it is his first book, his "maiden voyage" into both life and literature. There are other implications as well: the protagonist is like a maid—virgin and inexperienced—voyaging into the world.[6] We are informed that as a boy Denton was coddled by his mother, and the shock of her death charges the book's pages. Orphaned and inadequate, Denton is not up to the strenuous fagging at the preparatory school; he is never able to enter into it with any sense of camaraderie. When wet towels are flicked, he remembers, "I had been told that you could lift the skin off someone's back in this way. I always waited, half in horror, to see a ribbon of flesh come off" (48). His fellows continually taunt him, and he frequently goes into hiding. When some one calls him a "pretty boy" on the train, he hides in the lavatory for the journey's duration.

So he runs away from Repton (for which one might read "Rapeton" or "Representation"), making the first of three journeys in the book: Repton to Salisbury, England to Shanghai, and finally China to England—journeys that are both explorations and escapes. When he leaves Repton, he makes a sentimental journey to Salisbury, where he once had been with his mother. From there he goes to the house of his aunt, a mother substitute, hoping she will help him; but, when she does not agree that he should leave school, he feels betrayed. He finds he can't go back—only forward into the unknown. When his older brother arrives, he and the aunt discuss Denton in the third person, as if the boy had no mind of his own, no self worth consulting. They agree Denton must return to Repton, and the boy is terrified at the prospect. He equates life at Repton with the stream at the school, that stream in which "cold scum whirled under the bridge and reappeared with evil bubbles pushing through it" (35).

As a sign of Denton's higher aspirations—at his aunt's as well as at the school infirmary—he explores upper regions of the buildings—only to find empty rooms. Similarly, his searches for self and for meaning in life have led so far only to emptiness. An important part of Denton's search for his ultimate life role is the determination of his sexual identity, and early in the book it becomes apparent that the young man is not happily heterosexual. When he runs away from Repton, his first reaction is to disguise himself as a woman. At his cousin May's house, he wears a pair of her husband's pajamas; and, instead of feeling like a grown man or dwarfed, Denton felt "like a Chinese court lady" (21). Throughout the novel Denton is in perpetual flight from the female, and a misogynist point of view informs his every move. Early in the book, when he relates that "Two love-birds in the bay window were chattering and kissing and losing their feathers" (9-10), the loss of feathers is a telling detail: for Denton Welch, all heterosexual relations involved loss; the process of sexuality implies change and decay.

With the exception of memories of his mother, nearly every woman in *Maiden Voyage* is described in animalistic or predatory terms. The school nurse looks like a fox; Aunt Janet looks like a monkey "who grinned at me with her wide, prehistoric mouth" (45); Mrs. Wright "was like a greedy, sinewy spider" (105); and Denton's female cousin is described as wearing "cruel long hairpins" (22). Even the romantic myth of mermaids has no charm for him: "I imagined horrible little monkey faces and withered torsoes joined to disgusting, scaly tails" (108). He runs away from every woman who tries to get near him, including a prostitute who is after his body (26) and a young churchgoer who seeks his soul (92). The only woman with whom he was comfortable was his mother, now dead. Memories of her keep plaguing him, and one night he dreams of the Virgin Mary—of which more will be said later.

When Denton's father writes and invites him to China the following summer, the boy feels he can endure anything until the end of the term; and he agrees to return to school. But he dreads the return to that hearty male world in which he cannot compete because it has no place for the artist. The day he returns to Repton it is raining, and the spire of the school chapel appears to him "as slender as a sharpened pencil" (27), the symbolic phallus in the shadow of which he must work out his fate, and/or the diminished church whose former function he must now himself assume ("Work out your own salvation with fear and trembling").

Plunged once more into the life of the school, Denton's sexual confusion grows. When his pants are ripped off in gym class, he relishes the experience, describing the effect of the torn pants as a "flapping, divided skirt they had made for me" (49); and the word "skirt" is emblematic of ritual flaying. He also experiences ambivalent feelings toward the athletic youth Bradbourne, who beats him and treats him like an infant. Denton lets Bradbourne shave him, an act of symbolic emasculation; and he later sleeps in a chair beside him. And Denton both admires and hates Newman, Captain of House Games, for beating him with a cane. Denton's masochistic streak is rapidly being reinforced by the society he despises.

When Denton is later confined to the infirmary, he is embarrassed by physical contact with the nurse. Nevertheless, he senses that he and she are kindred spirits: they both abhor the roles thrust upon them by society: "She hated her uniform. She wanted to run in the fields, to trip over mole-hills and sprawl in the mud. She was a Peter Pan to herself" (36). Finally, to avoid loneliness at school, Denton takes up with the repellent Geoffrey, whose idea of humor is to "French kiss" him and then to call him a sissy. Geoffrey always carries his umbrella, a proud phallic symbol, and he uses it to prod others. At one point, he sticks "his umbrella between his legs like a battering ram" (85). Denton, on the other hand, does not wish to carry a rifle during Field Day maneuvers, thereby rejecting the aggressive role. In a significant scene in which Geoffrey and Denton encounter an unknown object in their path, Geoffrey skewers it on the ferrule of his umbrella and waves it at Denton, who is horrified to see it is a frog. His emotion upon seeing the frog impaled on the ferrule parallels his horror at the idea of sexual intercourse with a woman, whom he usually equates with loathsome animals or creatures. But his horror abates when he sees the object on the ferrule is only "an old, dead frog, dry and hard as leather" (44). Another interpretation of this highly charged scene is given in the next section of this chapter.

During another walk with Geoffrey, Denton observes a plant which fascinates him mightily. It "stood erect like a naked, aggressive phallus. It was white as if it had never been uncovered before" (83). In his excitement, Denton pulls at the plant and it breaks off "like a joint rotting in its socket." The plant was a Stink Horn, but when he puts it to his nose and breathes "in its filthiness deeply," the implications are obvious: young Denton is both fascinated and repelled by the symbol of male sexuality. Still later, after an older student makes a homosexual advance to him, Denton enjoys the squalor of the locker room: "The room was full of the nice smell of bodies, and gay shouts rang out. I sank down into the hot bath which twenty other people had already used. The thick, muddy waters stroked my flesh" (64). The verb "stroked" keys us to the emotions involved.

Maiden Voyage abounds with sexual symbols. One of the most significant and omnipresent is the slimy, weedy lake near the school grounds, a fetid and unpleasant yoni symbol. Another yoni is the gaping dyke into which he unhappily falls while on a chase. The fall caused him to feel as if he were cut in half, another manifestation of his state of symbolic emasculation. Everywhere Denton turns during the semester, he is affronted with sex, both natural and unnatural: he notices his aunt's dog practicing perversion on her cat (93); he observes a couple making love in the snow (97). The day after the second incident he returns to the site of the tryst to study the forms that the couple's figures had made in the snow. He gathers up the remains of the boy's cigarette —another broken phallus—"grey and wet now, falling away from the sodden strands of tobacco. I thought of it lighted and glowing, stuck between his teeth the night before" (98).

The return to the snowy love nest is the final episode in Part I of *Maiden Voyage*. True to his negative reaction on encountering the stinkweed phallus, the protagonist has decided he will never marry or have children. The only condition under which he deems marriage even thinkable would be if he "found a very old woman with plenty of money" (72). Such a union, of course, would preclude sexual intercourse and would also be a return to the mother figure.

In Part II the novel's emphasis shifts from Denton's struggle to preserve himself in school to his struggle to preserve himself in the transition between the groves of academe and the world beyond. Sailing toward China, he finds his anti-female feelings reaching a climax when he steals the greedy Mrs. Wright's box of chocolates and eats them all. This compulsive act, ultimately mixing pleasure with pain (he knows he will get a stomach ache as a result), is only one of many outrageous oral orgies in which he indulges: "It was like a communion feast. I was eating Mrs. Wright. Not for love but for hate, so that later she should be ejected from my body to go swimming down with the rest of the ship's sewage. I put large pieces in my mouth and savoured them deliciously" (105).

Later the ship's captain shows Denton the lamps in his cabin, lamps which are shaped like naked women; they disgust rather than excite the boy. At Columbo, he goes ashore and encounters a jewel-seller who spreads his wares on the ground before him and urges Denton to buy a gem for his "best lady." Denton admits he has none. "Then buy for your mother," the jeweler urges. "I have no mother," Denton shouts in anger. The jeweler has touched upon the nerve of the boy's problem. Later Denton has a nightmare, terrible in detail:

I once found myself in a narrow, squalid street where people jostled me and threw their filth into the gutters. Suddenly I came upon a woman lying on the pavement, her head propped against a wall. She was crying hopelessly and whining and groaning through her tears.

As I looked down my eyes focussed on a great steel hatpin. A shock of horror ran through me. The hat-pin pierced her left breast, the head and point appearing on each side of the globe of flesh. At her slightest movement milk spurted from the wounds, splashing her clothes and falling on her skin in white bubbles. (113-14)

This dream underlines Denton's fear of all feminine physiological functions, such as nursing and menstruation. His earlier dream of the Virgin Mary is related to his sacred memories of his mother, the one ideal woman with whom he attributes no unpleasant connotations; indeed, in his mind, her several childbirths may well have been immaculate conceptions. These dream visions of his mother as the Virgin Mary are compensatory in that they serve to strike a balance between his aversion to women in real life, in which he sees women as being as functional as rubber trees that ooze milk from their wounds. The hat-pin in the dream is a detail borrowed from his scrutiny of his cousin's attire, that lady in whose hands he felt betrayed.

By contrast, he admires on the ship the trim, athletic forms of Bob, the tutor, and the loutish sailor with whom Denton sunbathes atop the ship's cabin. There Denton lies naked and feels a child of nature, giving himself up to the heat and the vibrations (similar to the heroine of D. H. Lawrence's story, "Sun"). Denton, who closes his eyes, "felt as if I were strapped to the back of an enormous animal" (109). The ship itself seems to have become a phallus!

While aboard ship on the Red Sea, Denton begins to find an outlet for his repressed emotions: for the first time since he was nine years old he writes a poem. The act of creating poetry is strongly related to memories of his mother; his first poem was written for her while they were vacationing together in Switzerland. Through writing poetry he can once again summon up the blissful state of prelapsarian spontaneity. Now traveling to his father, from whom he has been estranged, he finds that poems come quickly and nearly perfectly. When he has started writing, he is far happier; for, in the creative moment, he can escape the world around him. When he sees on board some French-American children who are practically held captive by their parents, he wonders if they will ever escape. He himself is escaping, from school and from the world he has lived in up to that time. He has finally found release through art.

Section II concludes with Denton's arrival in China. His first encounter with another being is a warning from an English soldier who tells him to stay away from Chinese girls if he wishes to avoid a social disease; and once again horror of the female is awakened in him. He next travels to his father's apartment at the top of a tall tower—yet another phallus raising its head, and symbol of the strong father figure which he dreads and fears. Left alone in the apartment, he goes through boxes of his mother's jewels. Among them are several miniature paintings, of which he much prefers one of a little boy with a whip in his hands. The pretty boy and the whip presumably arouse his homosexual and masochistic tendencies. The section is climaxed by a dinner party at which Denton's father entertains several English and American friends. Denton is made to blush by the American woman's bit of doggerel about "Myrtle, the fertile turtle"; and he spends the remainder of the evening hating her for the crudeness of her allusions to feminine sexuality.

The action of the last and longest third of *Maiden Voyage* occurs totally in China. It is now the season of Denton's maturation: from the frozen, sterile fields of Repton, he has arrived where "the trees were sprouting with feathery, sickly green" (128). Once more a depressing yoni dominates

the scene; for, when Denton calls upon newly made friends,
he observes a deep swimming pool, empty and full of dead
and stagnant leaves. The friends are Vesta Fielding and her
husband Bob who live with Vesta's parents; indeed, she
had refused to marry him if she had had to live anywhere else.
She has, psychologically, remained a virgin—hence her
name; and the arrangement has rendered Bob ineffectual.
This marriage is not the best one for the impressionable
young Denton to have perceived in this season of his life.

When Denton arranges to travel into the interior with
an acquaintance of his father's, Vesta urges him to bring
back for her a head of Buddha in stone, iron, or bronze; and,
the female's wish for a head-figure is still another in a series
of symbolic emasculations. Early in the journey Denton sees
an elephant tusk that he would like to buy for himself; but,
because the price is too dear, he fails to acquire the totem
phallus. Later, at Nankin, when Denton observes a muscular
Chinaman pumping in his reed hut, he touches the man's
muscles and sees him as "a Roman boxer or athlete, glistening with oil" (141). Denton, who has come to idealize the
male physique, is overcome with admiration for any youth
or man of sturdy build. This incident expresses, of course,
the artist's envy of the "normal" person and also his appreciation of form.

When Denton and Mr. Butler, his traveling companion,
have dinner with the Consul, the official tells them of recent
trouble in which some Europeans in Nankin had been killed.
Immediately the boy's mind embarks upon a fantasy in
which "half-naked women ran down a hillside until they
were caught by brutal soldiers who raped them and then
plunged bayonets into their screaming bodies" (142). The
boy seems totally incapable of conceiving heterosexual relations in a tender light.

Related to the symbol of the dried-up swimming pool
is the dried-up garden which Denton's room overlooks, for
both convey infertility. Welch paints a symbolic landscape
with a heavy brush: the first morning Denton awakens
and goes for a walk in the country, and there he sees an object covered with flies. Bending closer to inspect it, he discerns in horror that the thing is a human head; and Welch

describes this naked, literal encounter: "The nose and eyes had been eaten away and the black hair was caked and grey with dust. Odd white teeth stood up like ninepins in its dark, gaping mouth. Its cheeks and shrivelled lips were plastered black with dried blood, and I saw long coarse hairs growing out of its ears" (151). This incident marks Denton's first encounter with death outside his immediate family. The apparent violence of the man's end unnerves him terribly; moreover, the severed head reinforces his sense of psychic emasculation.

Nor are Denton's misogynistic tendencies aided by the declamations of Roote's friend, the antique collector, who defames his wife with, "God preserve me from disgusting women, there's nothing worse in this world" (157). The collector contrasts the disgustingness of women with the pure, unearthly beauty of bronzes and porcelains. Denton himself is becoming a collector, accepting the world of art and antiques as a substitute for manhood.

As at Repton, everywhere Denton goes he seems to encounter sex in unnatural forms. The soldier he meets on the train platform makes overt sexual signs at him with his fingers (160). When Denton stays alone at the bungalow, one of the soldiers left to guard him reveals himself to be a *voyeur* (165). The man on the train and the scissors grinder both have syphillis (169, 170). He sees a woman dressed in man's clothing, a foreshadowing of what is to come (185). And the dogs play erotic games (191). All the while Denton is aware of his own physical and sexual inadequacies. He recalls how as a boy he had hated his black pony, an object which is desired by most young boys. Mrs. Murray, the arch-emasculator of the novel, points out that his voice still hasn't changed, thereby exacerbating his torment and reminding him he is still a child among adults (176).

At the country club, when a woman comments on his wearing sandals, he reacts defensively by wanting to push her into the pool so "that her skirts would float up and we should all see her suspenders pressing against her waxy, hairy, blue-veined thighs" (196). In contrast, Denton admires the swimming boy Crowther's "strong and lusty body." Denton later becomes envious of Dr. MacEwen's

body, too, and takes especial pleasure when MacEwen scrubs
his back for him—a scene that was possibly interpolated
into the story "When I Was Thirteen," for Denton's obsessions with sweets and sex are combined in this scene, as
they are in that story when Mrs. Murray hides her husband's
chocolates in the stool, thereby robbing him of his asser-
tive role by making him grovel about looking for the good-
ies (175).

Denton gradually becomes aware of loneliness as the
inescapable condition of man. When he returns to his cottage, he imagines that "I saw its tired, sick owner coming
home after his day's work and sinking into one of the dirty
chairs. I imagined him drinking his whiskey-and-soda, with
only the faked antiques for audience, then I heard him
running down the hollow-sounding passage and throwing
himself at last on the creaking bed" (175).

Despite his growing awareness, Denton is still not fully
an artist. On the trip to the interior, he tries to draw a beautiful pagoda he sees through the mist; but his drawing only
looks like a centipede (137), thereby revealing the limitations
of his artistic vision. He is very self-conscious about going
out with his paint box and easel, too. But, in a symbolic
scene, his school blazer is accidentally burned while serving
as a lampshade in a Chinese opium den and brothel—a
setting which might have served as the scene of his initiation
into manhood, had that been his desire. The burned blazer
ironically symbolizes the termination of all schoolboy ties
and concerns; for, from now on, he shall pursue his new artistic concerns. Later, in the streets, he sees the burial procession of a child, which could also be seen as a burial of
his own childhood.

The young man becomes bolder. He picks up a British
soldier and takes him to his father's flat, asserting himself
sexually as he has done artistically. The scene brings together two classes of British society for comparison and
contrast, but it is also a scene full of sexual implications.
The soldier tries to teach Denton how to smoke, but the
boy dislikes it, feeling the cigarette is "sticking out like a
bloody maypole" (204). Later, when Denton is sailing, his
boat is rammed—a violent sexual metaphor (211).

At the termination of his journey to the interior, Denton is aware of his failure to comply with Vesta's request for a Buddha head (male symbol). Instead, he returns with a small iron god which Vesta finds unsatisfactory. Denton also brought himself a broken jug, a vessel as incomplete as himself. He takes the broken jug to the home of a Mrs. Abercrombie, whose house is full of phalluslike lances and spears. Mrs. Abercrombie, though crippled, is the apotheosis of horrible womanhood for Denton; for her face is a blotched yellow and blue and red.

After all these wanderings the boy finally encounters someone whose friendship he feels could be meaningful. Predictably, it is not a fellow artist but another in his series of strong physical types. This man is a furniture-mover named Ernst who boxes in his leisure, and he presents a strong contrast to the frail antique-collecting Denton. When Denton hangs outside the window of the building where Ernst boxes, he becomes the voyeur rather than the object of one as he was earlier in the journey. When he is apprehended by the boxer and invited to a bout, Denton takes a violent beating from Ernst; and he masochistically enjoys it: "I lay on the bolsters, trying to define to myself the flavour of the blood, while he wiped my face and neck. The coolness was delicious. I hoped that my nose would not stop bleeding. The towel and my handkerchief were soaked to a wonderful red. What a pity it doesn't last! I thought. My lip was beginning to feel inflated and leathery" (226).

When Denton now sunbathes, it is no longer as it was aboard the ship heading for China, when he felt purified by the sun. He sunbathes naked now, and large pieces of soot blow from the chimneys onto his body; the soot leaves long black smears on his skin. His attraction for Ernst has changed him; he is tainted. When Ernst deserts him, Denton picks up an American marine who takes him to a dance hall where the bawdy crowd tries to pull the trousers off a sailor.

Denton becomes increasingly misogynistic and is embarrassed before anything female. When the girl Ruth starts to explain menstruation to him, he jumps up in confusion. When Elaine invites him to dive underwater between her legs, he "had a terror of being caught between them" (241).

His attitude toward marriage is further demonstrated in parable form by the tale of the American woman who marries the man Charles who dies shortly thereafter in the night. The incident is related to that of the shedding love birds explicated earlier. Heterosexual love clearly equals death or destruction for Denton.

All these related events climax in the scene in which Denton is left alone in Vesta's room. Here he dresses himself as a girl, not out of need to disguise himself—as he did early in the novel, when he locked himself in the train lavatory—but simply because he now wishes to. He dresses and paints himself with rising excitement: "By the time I had finished, the profession to which I belonged was quite unmistakable. I felt an urgent need to go out in my new disguise. It was too good to be wasted" (243). He climbs down the roof and minces about the streets in high drag.

On a successive evening Denton attends a night club. He feels uncomfortable in his evening clothes and thinks longingly of the freedom he felt wearing Vesta's dresses. At the club he dances with a beefy woman named Belle, representative of all belles. She takes the lead when they dance, and she accuses him of being too passive—a remark we may interpret as underscoring the theme of the novel. He leaves the club and encounters the same soldier in the street that he had entertained in his father's apartment. Together they sing Brahms' lullaby in the streets, perhaps out of nostalgia for the innocence of childhood.

When Vesta later deliberately kicks a program-seller in the opera house, the poor man howls in falsetto as if she has castrated him—which, in spirit, all females in the novel have done to all males. At another time Denton drinks out of a cup which shows "Cupid being let out of a rabbit-hutch by the Empress Josephine" (274); and we once more have the vision of the male held captive by the female. At this stage of his development, Denton's appetite, long related to his sexual appetite, asserts itself aggressively. In a statement fraught with Freudian overtones, he declares, "I seemed to have a great need which I must satisfy by taking things into myself" (281).[7] The time is now winter, and the block of flats which had looked so white and glittering in the summer are now yellow and stained, the colors of decadence. The young corn of last year now is nothing but an icy pile of leaves. Everything has changed; and, when Denton loses his coat during a chase by the law, after helping drunken soldiers pass sentry illegally, he is shedding the skin of his former self, the self that had never before broken the laws of society. This book has traced his progression from one state to another and finally to a more advanced one. The burning of the blazer and the loss of the topcoat marked the shedding of each self.

The novel ends with a series of sordid images, including the boy's finding a prophylactic in the storage room and his observing two homosexual soldiers in a bar. Finally, he has an argument with his father prior to his departure for England. It is decided the boy can go to art school, but Denton is upbraided by his father for attempting to take his mother's belongings with him without permission. The gulf between father and son is widened irreparably.

Denton's maiden voyage is ended when he says farewell to Vesta, his best and only platonic friend. Then he sits down to lunch on the ship beside a Mrs. Morgan, whose tea service he already has bought at auction because she is bankrupt. The two of them "tried to talk as if neither of us had lost anything" (303). Clearly, the boy is psychologically bankrupt; he has, on his maiden voyage, lost his boyhood, his father, and his innocence.

III *Mythic Implications*

Denton Welch was not a scholar, as he himself admitted; and the host of myths and folk tales he ordered in the symbols of *Maiden Voyage* were probably purely spontaneous products of his psyche. In any event, the logic and the deeds of the protagonist follow the standard path of the mythological journey of the hero. A leading myth scholar, Joseph Campbell, has distilled the monomyth as follows:

The mythological hero, setting forth from his commonday hut or castle, is lured, carried away, or else voluntarily proceeds, to the threshold of adventure. There he encounters a shadow presence that guards the passage. The hero may defeat or conciliate this power and go alive into the kingdom of the dark (brother-battle, dragon-battle; offering, charm), or be slain by the opponent and descend in death (dismemberment, crucifixion). Beyond the threshold, then, the hero journeys through a world of unfamiliar yet strangely intimate forces, some of which severely threaten him (tests), some of which give magical aid (helpers). When he arrives at the nadir of the mythological round, he undergoes a supreme ordeal and gains his reward. The triumph may be represented as the hero's sexual union with the goddess-mother of the world (sacred marriage), his recognition of the father-creator (father atonement), his own divinization (apotheosis); or again— if the powers have remained unfriendly to him—his theft of the boon he came to gain (bride-theft, fire-theft); intrinsically it is an expansion of consciousness and therewith of being (illumination, transfiguration, freedom). The final work is that of the return. If the powers have blessed the hero, he now sets forth under their protection (emissary); if not, he flees and is pursued (transformation flight, obstacle flight). At the return threshold the transcendental powers must remain behind; the hero re-emerges from the kingdom of dread (return, resurrection). The boon that he brings restores the world (elixir).[8]

I suggest that Welch's first novel is unconsciously structured upon most of the key actions and images of the mythological hero's adventure. Like the composite hero of ancient myths, the hero of *Maiden Voyage* is a youth of exceptional gifts— in this case, artistic ability. The protagonist's journey into the interior of China—the world womb, the belly of the whale—is the inward passage of the mythological hero, a journey ultimately into the depths of his own awakening soul. China, that mysterious land of impossible delights and cruelties, is the symbolic scene, as well as the literal one, of Denton's rites of passage.

Welch divided *Maiden Voyage* into three sections, which we might label Call to Adventure (Part I), Crossing the First Threshold (Part II), and Initiation and Return (Part III); and the book's title refers to the hero's first major adventure, voyaging forth into the world defenseless, inexperienced. Denton's feelings of uselessness early in the novel signal the hero's call to adventure, the first stage of the mythological journey. When he runs away from school, he crosses the threshold by expressing his refusal of common destiny in favor of shaping his own, contrary to the expectations of society. By taking the wrong train, the one to Salisbury rather than to Repton, he really takes the right one—at least, the one which is right for him. His call to adventure is the artistic calling, and the cathedrals he visits in Salisbury are symbols of the union of art and religion. Also, in his encounter with the dead frog (death), and the drunken man (Nausea), his revulsion at life is dramatized. He is like the young Prince Gautama Sakyamuni of legend, the future Buddha, whose father had protected him from all sight of old age, sickness, and death until the Prince sought new experiences and ventured forth to find them. This is the moment of destiny at which Denton also had arrived—the moment of the call to adventure when "destiny has summoned the hero and transferred his spiritual center of gravity from within the pole of his society to a zone unknown."[9]

It is significant, then, that Denton approaches his cousin May Bolton's house through an entrance between two stucco lions (17). The lions are guardians (gargoyles) which warn the hero of the real dangers ahead during the quest for selfhood and individualism. Denton is undaunted by warnings, however; he is eager to do battle with his dragon, which in his case is the society of which he finds himself a part, male-dominated Western civilization. His readiness, "ripeness," for adventure is symbolized by his exploration of the empty rooms at his aunt's house during his leisure. But he immediately encounters obstacles to his plans for independence.

There are, first, the literal obstacles of his aunt's and brother's opposition to his leaving school (even his brother's friends taunt him), causing him to engage in a Brother-battle. Second, there are the psychological obstacles of the tainted memory of his mother, recalling in literature both Oedipus and Hamlet, men for whom women have become the symbols of defeat rather than of victory. Denton, who feels this revulsion, becomes the novitiate hero who no longer can "rest in innocence with the goddess of the flesh; for she is become the Queen of sin."[10] The stinkhorn episode, related in Section II of this chapter, illustrates this revulsion: it is Denton's refusal of the call to assume the adult male function in the life process. Even the stench of the phallic-shaped plant communicates his vision of the repellent nature of the sexual function. There is ambivalence present in this symbol, however; it has the numinosity of an archetype, at once fascinating and repellent.

A prominent feature of all heroes of legend, folk tale, and myth is the infant exile and return; and Denton's long semesters at boarding school could be viewed as his exile. Furthermore, many myths supplement this theme of exile with that of the hero's status of being orphaned; and Denton's loss of his mother and his relative ignorance of his father qualify him as a symbolic orphan. The plot of *Maiden Voyage* moves toward the same conclusion as the monomyth, the return of the exiled hero who, after a long period of obscurity, can finally reveal his true character.

Before embarking on the long voyage, Welch's protagonist must suffer a detour: he is forced to return to school until the term's end. While he is at his aunt's, he begins experimenting, hoping to find some relief from life as he is living it. He drinks from all the bottles of her medicine cabinet, as if they are magic potions. When he returns to school, he tries smoking and drinking as well; but he enjoys neither. A visit to church fails, since the door is locked; and the locked door signifies that the conventional and traditional religious path is closed to the hero. It clearly is a time for crossing the threshold and entering the world of art and solitude.

At school, Denton fulfills the mythic hero's destiny for dismemberment or crucifixion. He is flogged; and, during the act, his cut trousers come to resemble the flayed flesh of a sacrificial victim. In most ancient religious rites, flaying denoted transformation to a better state and, therefore, renewal and rebirth.[11] Rebirth is also recalled with imagery reminiscent of the piercing of Christ's side with a sword, when Denton is symbolically crucified as Geoffrey impales the frog on his umbrella ferrule; Denton is the frog; almost, we might say, the Frog Prince—since he also is a rejected youth who is, in reality, the son of a rich man and the possessor of a beautiful spirit.[12] While marking time at school, Denton encounters a couple making love in the snow; and his observing the couple on a bed of snow is also significant: water in a frozen state. Through the ages water has been a universal symbol of life and possibilities. That the snow-water possibilities are frozen (arrested) seems an unconscious statement or recognition that, for him, normal male-female congress is impossible.

Another initiation, as well a fulfillment of the mythic passage of the hero through the Symplegades, is the clashing opposites of earthly existence (in this case, male and female). Finally, the Hero-Christ-Frog-Prince Denton is abducted when his father sends for him to go to China. He answers the call and crosses the first threshold. Symbolically, he buys new clothes, knowing a change in him will occur with the journey; and he reminds us of Christ's admonition that we must not put new wine in old bottles.

The night-sea journey symbolizes the unknown depths of unconsciousness which the hero is to explore. The literal voyage to China on the Red Sea begins to form a link with the unconscious that prompts Denton to write poetry, become the artist, and feel truly happy for the first time. Once beyond the threshold, our hero journeys through a Wonder World. China, for Denton as for all men, is the land of wonder, mystery, dreams; of the foreign, the inscrutable—the unconscious. It is significant that Denton, the potential artist, begins to feel most himself in the East. Having rejected the West, the land of consciousness, insensitivity, and male aggression, he journeys to the interior of China,—that is, into the passivity of Self.

He is happier, but the threats or tests begin almost immediately. The climate for testing is apparent in the image of the feathery, sickly, green, sprouting trees already cited—an image combining both the promise of new birth and the possibility of the failure of his quest. Among the tests are the many disquieting scenes he is forced to view: his encounter with the yellow, diseased dogs; the huge granite beasts in the garden—mythic, dreamlike forms, composing a landscape of the unconscious; and the natives with their loads of human manure, a symbol deriving from the ancient alchemical idea that from the lowest (excrement, urine) come the highest or spiritual truths, and one which, when comprehended, can teach Denton that nothing in life must be rejected.[13]

Denton's magical aid comes in the form of a helper, his father's friend Mr. Butler, whose name is significant: a butler is one who ushers in; and Mr. Butler serves as a Charon figure for Denton, for he assists the boy over the figurative River Styx in the underground. Mr. Butler leads Denton into the interior, to the coal-mines of deepest China, where Denton has his deepest experiences.

His new friend Vesta is also appropriately named. She is goddess of the hearth, the one who is trapped in infancy and remains perpetually at home. Rather than accompany Denton on his heroic journey, she plays Penelope to his Odysseus, remains behind, and instructs him to return with a boon, a stone Buddha head. Ultimately, he fails to fulfill her request, bringing instead something else; and this individual choice underscores the principle that each must make his own journey in life and not depend on others to get what he wants.

Additional trials, real or symbolic, which lie in Denton's path during his own quest for self are the guardian lions at the tomb (who hold fast to the secret of death); the gargoyles (which Campbell would tell us are "the threshold guardians to ward away all incapable of encountering the higher silences within . . . they illustrate the fact that the devotee at the moment of entry into a temple undergoes a metamorphosis");[14] and his horrifying encounter of the severed head, a vision combining both life and death. This experience dramatizes the horror of a confrontation with the holy mystery, the deathshead; and here Hamlet confronts Yorick's skull. In this encounter, Denton must confront the basic fact of life, after which his world view is altered and even the grasses appear to him "dry and sharp as knives" (152). The "hardness" or objectivity of myth or dogma is good in that the individual can lose his ego in contemplating it and, in so doing, become part of the life-process rather than a resistor of it. The protean hero becomes himself, hardened and objectified.

The dangers of exploring the unconscious depths are

dramatized several times, once on a symbolic level when Denton loses himself outside the gates, like Daedalus lost in the maze of self; and again on a literal level when a man and his wife are murdered by antiforeign demonstrators. At this point in the enactment of the monomyth, Denton as hero would have to steal the boon or elixer because the powers are unfriendly to him. Yet he clearly must come to terms with himself. His visit to the sick in the hospital and his encounters with old people, like those of the Gautama Buddha, have pricked his consciousness too deeply. The visions of old age, infirmity, and death are too real. He knows he is without hope unless he obtains some magic talisman.

The descent into Hell occurs when Denton enters the manure-filled cattle car with Mr. Butler assisting. The soldiers who stop the car, appropriately, are described as grinning "like devils in a Medieval picture" (179). Returning from the descent, Denton fails to secure the boon Vesta demanded; instead of the stone head of Buddha (symbol of godhood or divinity), he returns bearing a small iron god for her and a broken jug for himself. These are telling symbols: the iron god harkens back to Anthroparion, the little leaden man of the Zosimos vision as related by C. G. Jung, as well as other figures of mythology, "the metallic men who dwell in the mines, the crafty dactyls of antiquity, the homunculi of the alchemists, and the gnomic throng of hobgoblins, brownies, gremlins, etc."[15] Whichever, the figure is of a lesser god rather than the grand Buddha that Vesta had requested and expected. It is a symbol of that which is attainable by most men in this life, rather than the unattainable state of divinity.

The broken jug, on the other hand, is a symbol of Denton himself, a broken vessel of the spirit. Just as his attempted rescue fails to save the puppy from being killed or sold for stew, so too does he fail in all other respects to fulfill the role of hero. Most especially he fails in his quest for full, human, male maturity and atonement with his father. And, because he is unable to consummate the sacred marriage with the goddess residing in every woman, he must himself assume the female role for satisfaction. This sexual inversion is ultimately responsible for the limitation of his art:

his poems and paintings contain distortions of the female element. (That this was equally true of the real Welch's art may be discerned from a study of his paintings, such as "Nina," reproduced in *A Last Sheaf*, a grotesque portrait of a lady with exposed and unnatural breasts.) At the conclusion of *Maiden Voyage*, Denton becomes the broken jug; his restriction of consciousness prevents his becoming whole, or his pouring himself out for others fully and satisfactorily in his art. Upon his return to the threshold, it is clear that the powers have not wholly blessed the hero.

IV   *The Christ Archetype*

Finally, *Maiden Voyage* abounds with birth imagery and biblical allusions, and the two are often inseparable, thereby suggesting that the author saw his young protagonist as a possible Christ figure. "The long, silent slipping through the Suez Canal" is Denton's birth or rebirth. Much is made of his sleeping naked, the state in which one is born into the world. During the trip he feels seasick, and in the water imagery there is a suggestion of amniotic fluids. We recall earlier at school how the boy had climbed into a deep hole in the ground behind the gym and had merely sat there, thinking. In his voyage, he retreats to other womblike enclosures as well, specifically to the jail cell and to the train lavatory, where he feels safer.

Denton's first rebirth occurs when he escapes to his aunt's house. When he arrives, he washes himself very thoroughly after the long journey, much as a doctor would bathe a baby (19). While at his aunt's, he dreams of the Virgin Mary, a dream no doubt reminding him of his mother as well as having religious connotations. He attends a Christmas service; and he studies, on another occasion, a picture of the Nativity. When he is forced to return to school, he reads a passage from the Bible, and again it is significantly a passage about the Nativity. The author seems to be establishing parallels between the protagonist's several rebirths—to selfhood, to art, and finally to carnality—and the birth of Christ. It is perhaps no accident, then, that the art-school building, in which Denton first awakens to art, had formerly been an ox stable. The new Denton (his new Self) is literally born in a stable. Later Denton identifies himself strongly with the bearded beggar "who looked like Jesus" (192) and whom villagers persecute and taunt. Denton gives the man all his week's pocket money in an act of Christian charity, then returns to take back a dollar. In doing so, he betrays the Christ figure for coins, symbolic of the biblical thirty pieces of silver. (See Welch's story, "The Judas Tree," in *Brave and Cruel,* for a similar theme.) The boy in turn betrays his own nature.

Later in the novel when Denton becomes more worldly-wise, Christianity is mocked. He blasphemously thinks "how nice it would be to have burnt sacrifices offered to me when I am dead" (190), a thought which reveals his pre-occupation. Ultimately, we recall the mocking image of the chamberpot on top of the broken village cross at Repton, a symbol of the visceral rather than the spiritual. Denton's supersophistication deprives him of any claim to spirituality he might have had.

These few references should make clear the psychological position of Denton's Christ figure in *Maiden Voyage.* As C. G. Jung has theorized, Christ exemplifies the archetype of the Self, a glorified man, unspotted by sin, a correspondent of the first Adam before the Fall.[16] *Maiden Voyage* is Denton Welch's spiritual odyssey, a search for oneness, in which certain spontaneous symbols of the Self became indistinguishable from a God-image. "This is in exact agreement with the empirical findings of psychology, that there is an ever-present archetype of wholeness which may easily disappear from the purview of consciousness or may never perceived at all until a consciousness illuminated by conversion recognizes it in the figure of Christ."[17] Whether this archetype was consciously manufactured by Welch (he stated that he wished to create "biblical symbols") or subconsciously imposed, it is present and makes the book even more effective. Whichever interpretation the reader ultimately assigns to *Maiden Voyage,* we can say of that book what Henry James said of Whitman's Civil War letters to Peter Doyle: "The beauty of the natural is here, the overflow of the man's life in the deadly dry setting." This overflow of aspiration and hope characterizes Welch's writing from *Maiden Voyage* forward.

CHAPTER 3

In Youth Is Pleasure

I *The Sexual Search*

WHEN Welch's second novel was published two years after *Maiden Voyage,* several disappointed American critics carped that the manuscript of *In Youth Is Pleasure* must have been resurrected from the bottom of Welch's trunk; and they called the craft and the vision inferior to those evident in the first book. A critical charge often heard in response to second novels, it is also one that neither biographical fact nor cool critical judgment can support in Welch's case. *In Youth Is Pleasure* is definitely a later product of Welch's imagination; his craft is a more mature one; the writing is tighter and harder, more incisive and sure; and the the language is more sophisticated. However, as Maurice Cranston observes, Welch "kept the trick of lighting up a passage of conventional narrative with one of his arresting child's images," as in the following description:

He walked slowly into the dark water and lay down flat. His exultation passed into a more sober delight. Water always soothed him. He felt calm and peaceful. As he floated he felt the sun hot on his face, and on the parts of his chest and arms which were still above water. The rest of his body was tingling with cold.

"I'm like one of those Baked Alaskas," he thought, "one of those lovely puddings of ice cream and hot sponge."[1]

In passages such as this, in a book little over half the length of *Maiden Voyage,* Welch again gives a provocative examination of the secret life of a sensitive youth.

Hamilton Basso, the late American Southern novelist, considered this book's protagonist "the most desperately miserable English schoolboy who ever found his way into print,"[2] an accolade we might have thought would already have been retired by the protagonist of *Maiden Voyage*. This time, however, the hero is named Orvil Pym, not Denton Welch; but they are the same character, in background, and in spirit. Both are lonely searchers given to the wildest flights of fancy, and their situation is also the same: as in *Maiden Voyage*, we have the youthful errant scholar's quest for self-knowledge in an alien world which is at once thrilling and frightening. In the first novel, the hero conducted his quest, or voyage, in China; in *In Youth Is Pleasure*, the boy and his two older brothers vacation with their father in a grand hotel on the Thames.[3] The novel's action is more limited; the time span, more condensed. But its greatest defect lies in the author's choice of the third-person point of view; it demanded an attitude to the external world which the solipsistic Welch could not sustain, as Maurice Cranston notes.[4] Nevertheless, as rich in symbol and theme as Welch's first novel, the second lacks only the mythic implications to elevate it to the same level of complexity. In this work, mythic symbols have been displaced by consciously Gothic ones, and unconscious sexual ones.

In regard to my interpretation of the symbolism of this novel: some readers may think I overemphasize that old stock-in-trade of Freudian literary critics, the sexual symbol. To such readers I can only reply that, in *In Youth Is Pleasure*, Welch's quest for self-discovery is construed almost entirely in sexual terms. (Later, in *A Voice Through a Cloud*, the sexual is displaced by the Existential, additional proof that Welch did grow from book to book, despite some critics' avowal that each new book was a rewriting of the last.) Symbolism, as we know, is one of the most important forms of expression of the unconscious; and Welch's sexual anxieties seem most certainly to have surfaced in the multitude of broken columns, threatening spears, snapped-off knives, and bottomless lakes and swimming pools which decorate the psychescape of all his novels, but especially that of *In Youth Is Pleasure*. His character, Orvil Pym, seems to possess a "one-track mind," and his sexual fears appear to reflect Welch's at the time of composition. The creative process, for all artists, begins with a relaxation of ego control. In this book Welch not only seems aware of the relaxation/regression but also seemingly willed it. Certainly, the framework given his symbols is consciously Gothic, as if the wild, uncivilized, and unrestrained conventions of Gothic literature gave point to his own wild sexuality.

The situation of the novel is overtly Oedipal and homosexual. Welch dedicated it "To Rosalind Bassett" without identifying her as his mother, without mention of the fact she had been dead nearly twenty years, and—interestingly enough—without appending her married name of Welch; but perhaps this is appropriate, because she was so alive in his mind, the bride of his imagination. The end papers which Welch drew especially to decorate the novel are also illuminating; for, executed in pen and ink in his somewhat *"art nouveau"* style, the designs are dominated by a broken spear crossing a totally devoured fish—that is, a broken male sex symbol crosses a broken female symbol. The drawing graphically announces that the novel concerns aborted sexuality. The facing end paper, which reinforces this theme, portrays a long snake (phallus) that is devouring an egg (yoni).

Orvil is every bit as high-strung and emotional as was the hero of *Maiden Voyage.* He is so sensitive that he twists or magnifies every event out of all reasonable proportion. He is also extremely lonely. His mother is dead and he barely knows his father, a self-centered man who drinks too much, who has taken opium on occasion, and who persists in calling the self-conscious boy alternately "Microbe" and "Maggot." The second name is especially unfortunate in view of Orvil's preoccupation with his mother's death and his persistent visions of her in a deathly state. His father will not even allow the boy's mother's name to be mentioned between them. Orvil's loneliness is exacerbated rather than assuaged by the presence of his two brothers during holidays since he simultaneously admires and resents the poise of one and the masculinity of the other. (The autobiographical parallels here are obvious.)

As a result of his familial alienation, Orvil wanders about and indulges in all manner of daydreams, the details of which could supply Kraft-Ebbing with another lifetime's work. Fifteen-year-old Orvil's imagination is far more erotic than was the protagonist's of *Maiden Voyage,* for then "Denton" of that book was fanciful, not libidinous. On the other hand, Orvil's sleep is disturbed by highly sexual dreams in which he sees himself "lying full length in an enormous open wound"; or, having regressed to the infantile stages, he is lost underneath huge flowers composed of "grotesquely enlarged diamonds" which wave about "on long gold wires" (13).[5] The open wound, of course, can suggest the vagina; the pendulous diamonds and the long wires, a phallus. Wishing to remain a child, and remembering always his youthful bliss with his mother, Orvil is terrified by the prospect of adult sexuality. He prays that his voice will not change, that his face will remain beardless.

Before coming to the hotel, Orvil, in a highly symbolic scene, found a steel-lined athletic supporter in his aunt's attic. He had stripped and strapped on the supporter, but he found it "much too large," a contrast emphasizing his youthful sexual apparatus and his increasing psychic fears of sexual inadequacy. Nevertheless, the supporter in time made him feel "very safe" and, while wearing it, he gave himself his first shave: only when protected by a steel-lined jock does he dare to brandish a razor. In his mind, the act of shaving is equated with growing up; and growing up is equated with castration, signified by the losing of one's voice. Wearing the supporter is Orvil's youthful way of protecting his childlike sexuality from the assaults of the world.

Sexuality is so central to this novel that the opening image is, in fact, that of a huge yoni. The hotel to which Orvil's womanless family retreats is located on a neglected artificial lake which is completely surrounded by brambles. The lake seems a vagina symbol, again, the brambles emblems of wiry pubic hair. But more appropriately, the brambles are the difficult obstacles the tender Orvil must overcome to realize the yoni and achieve heterosexuality. Among these barriers is his solitary pleasure in masturbation, which he enacts several times during the book; and the reader should bear in mind that Welch was writing twenty-five years before Mr. Philip Roth and his *Portnoy's Complaint* made masturbation an accepted subject for literature.

Another key image early in the novel is the Peach Melba which Orvil orders at dinner, despite his father's disapproval. Orvil views the "buttock-like shape of the fruit" with its red and white sauce as looking like "a celluloid cupid doll's behind" which "has burst open and is pouring out lovely snow and great big clots of blood" (11). On the first level, this image is telling one because the cupid doll (kewpie-doll) is a traditional symbol for idealized infancy. Here the boy views the golden, fair-haired doll as being broken and spilling its blood and viscera. His youth, then, has been violently damaged. But this is not the only significance of the Peach Melba. At a later point in the novel where Orvil is trying to sleep, he can only summon images of his dead mother. In a half-dream, he sees her rising from the grave, wearing a "tousled peach night gown" (21). The Peach Melba, then, is at once the image of his youth destroyed and the Oedipal image of his mother.

More so than in any other book by Denton Welch, the writing in *In Youth Is Pleasure* has an unreal quality; for the incidents seem part dream, part memory, part reality. The prose is well-suited to the psychological state of the protagonist, as when Orvil is so supremely unhappy and confused that he sees the hotel "as a terrifying labyrinth, with the minotaur waiting for him somewhere in the dark" (19), an allusion that confirms that Welch was cognizant of certain myths. In Orvil's explorations about the hotel grounds, he encounters a deserted cottage in the dingle, to which he is later to return. He also becomes aware of the pillars on each side of the gate to the hotel. Orvil notes one has "a broken spear-tip" jutting out, a portent of his broken sexuality which is to come.

When the action of the novel moves to the scene of the Searchlight Tattoo, a military spectacle, the song leader there is described as having pectoral muscles "so relaxed and overlaid with fat . . . they looked like a pretty adolescent girl's breasts" (27). The androgynous character of the songleader renders him reminiscent of Tiresias, the Theban

soothsayer of mythology (whom T.S. Eliot also used as a symbolic spectator in *The Waste Land,* and in whose body "the
two sexes meet," to quote Eliot).[6] Welch's big-breasted song
leader, the androgyne, is a symbol central to *In Youth Is
Pleasure,* one that underscores the ambivalence and bisexuality of young Orvil.

When the performance of the Tattoo begins, we are greeted,
in contrast, by a procession of proud drum majors and gladi-
ator-type young men draped in leopard skins. These epitomes
of healthy young masculinity are led by "a delicate-stepping
wicked little goat, with its beautiful powdered hair blowing
freely in the wind, leading all these hundreds of meekly
obeying men in arrogant scarlet cloth, gold braid and fur"
(28). The goat is an obvious Pan-figure, and Welch seems to
be saying that the majority of men blindly follow Pan without
questioning the true nature of their sexuality. Orvil, sitting
in the bleachers, mentally blocks this vision. In his mind's
eye he employs the whole regiment to practice sodomy on
the goat, an act agreeable to his imagination, until the
goat-Pan is killed.

After returning to the hotel, Orvil's next meaningful
experience is to encounter two boys and a man who are
canoeing on the river. They are tanned, they sing lustily, and
they present an image of idealized youth and manhood.
The canoe they paddle is scarlet, the color of the life force.
They wear stout leather belts from which dangle heavy
knives with handles of rough horn. The heavy knives are
male totems, and we recall earlier in the novel Orvil's experience while attempting to force the cottage window with
his small pen knife: the blade had snapped and cut him
badly. Orvil's male totem is inadequate, then, and he cannot employ it satisfactorily.

Orvil, who is immediately envious of the natural life this
trio leads, resolves to rent himself a canoe, as if that will
give him his freedom. Having rented one, he also buys a
scarlet bathing-slip, which he sees as "a very potent symbol—something very free, daring" (47). Instead of his pallid
intellectualism, Orvil is attempting to actively substitute
the natural life, symbolized by the color of blood in the slip.
He paddles to the spot where he knows the man and the two

boys are; he spies upon them; and he hears the man (who appears to be mildly sadistic and perhaps latently homosexual) abuse the boys physically as well as verbally. Orvil becomes so excited by this scene that he finds a solitary place in the woods and again masturbates.

From this point Orvil's imagination revolves about the man in the woods and his young companions. The man in the red canoe is an aggressive life force afloat on the river of life, and the red canoe is perhaps an angry phallus. More important is the fact that the man seems both father and mother to his young charges. Since Orvil's mother is dead and since his father is indifferent, the man in the woods is also a possible parent substitute. To prepare himself for his encounter with the man, Orvil studies a book on physical culture borrowed from the hotel library; and his sexual fantasies become so increasingly phallus-oriented that even the dessert cakes on the dining room tray appear phallic to him. The sexuality and sadism of the camper have appealed to Orvil, though he does not consciously acknowledge this fact. He only knows that he has viewed the open life and found it to his liking.

Thus Welch has successfully juxtaposed two distinct manners of life in this novel: the hotel up the river at which Orvil stays represents the suprarefined life of the English upperclass, where everyone is decorous and dresses for dinner; and the summer camp down river represents the free life, an existence where the male wears hardly any clothes at all and builds fires to cook his rude meals. To Orvil, the hotel is just another institution, like the school, which he detests so thoroughly but to which he knows he must return at summer's end.

Orvil next enters a period of confusion. He steals a lipstick from a store—an object both phallic and feminine, that underscores once more his androgynous nature. Then he seeks solace by visiting country churches (we recall his mother's ardent religiousity); but he finds the churches to be cold comfort. In one, he kisses the cool brass figure on a lady's tomb. His fancies fly first to rings which may still adorn the lady's skeletal fingers and then to thoughts frankly necrophilic. That the dead lady and her brass likeness are a surrogate for Orvil's mother is probable. His mother's memory and her rings always accompany one another: in one flashback, we are told Orvil had taken the signet ring off his mother's little finger and tied it in his hair, knotting it with two of his long curls in a sort of Oedipal marriage ceremony. After that, he and his mother had very ceremoniously eaten a pickle each from a plate, an act symbolic of the willful destruction of the phallus. In this context, the later church scene, one in which rings and the dead lady whose image he kisses are entwined, is yet another manifestation of Orvil's Oedipal fixation. The scene concludes with his getting drunk on communion wine and being frightened by a looming phallus, the church tower.

Finding no release in church-going, Orvil begins to withdraw from the world and to entertain a death wish; for he desires to have no body, no vestiges of manhood. Once he shuts himself inside a wardrobe; another time, he pulls himself into the bottom drawer of a large dresser and, in so doing, recalls tales of Chinese torture boxes in dungeons, boxes just large enough for a wretched prisoner to crouch in. Orvil imagined that "he was locked in a box forever, lying in his own excrement, screaming to straighten his legs and back, never being able to" (64). This vision is suggestive of a difficult or even a still birth, and Orvil's fear of never being capable of straightening his legs and leaving the box parallels his ambivalent fears of leaving the childlike state.

Aside from the excremental image, of which this is only one of many in the novel, it is significant to note the recurrence of fetal positions, both real and imaginary, which Orvil assumes during the short book: in the canoe, in the wardrobe, in the drawer, under the altar of the church, and especially in his brother's sportscar, where Orvil rides crouched in the box at the back with his head under a rug (68). Each of these episodes is a symbolic return to the womb. Later Orvil even expresses intrigue with the world inside of shoes, an obsession combining his desire to withdraw with his delight in the miniature: "It's always mysterious inside shoes; like a dark cave. No light ever reaches the end. You can only feel along the walls blindly" (116).

Orvil next unites withdrawal with masochism. He locks

himself in the musicians' cloakroom beneath the hotel ball-
room stage, strips, and flagellates himself with a leather
strap. Enjoying it, he recalls the floggings he had witnessed
and experienced at school.[7] In his masochism, he is inflicting punishment he would rather have the camper in the
woods mete out to him. Subsequently, he goes outdoors and
wraps a chain about himself, pretending he is a slave—another manifestation of his desire to serve abjectly the camper.

In a shop, Orvil sees a work bag made from a baby armadillo's body: "The eyes were heavy-lidded, shriveled and
blind; the tiny feet dried and curled into bird claws. He put
it down and turned away, feeling sick" (73). The bag is an
objective correlative for Orvil himself, for not only was the
life of the creature halted in its early stage, like Orvil's, but
all the vitals have been evacuated; the entire body of the
armadillo now is hollow and lined with cherry satin, and
Orvil, likewise, is hollow. He knows he must seek the man
in the woods to realize somehow his own, essential identity.

He spies on the man twice before actually confronting
him. Once Orvil reluctantly goes canoeing with his brothers,
and the awkward paddling of the Pym boys is contrasted with
the smooth strokes of the three campers; for, unlike them,
Orvil and his brothers are out of rhythm with nature. Another time the camper and his young cohorts are eating when
Orvil spies on them; and much is made of the boys' "playing
with their sausages." That Orvil saw the sausages in a sexual light rather than a culinary one is reinforced by his later
chanting a bawdy limerick about the sausage-loving lady
from Twickenham (171). Sausages, pickles, lady fingers—always the phallus asserts itself.

Finally Orvil plays for a third time peeping Tom and is
discovered. He finds he cannot face the man, and turns
to run. After a chase, the two finally encounter each other;
and the man reveals himself to be a London headmaster
attached to a mission that requires him to bring various
campers to the site for outings. When he gruffly takes charge
of Orvil and orders him about, Orvil, having earlier day-
dreamed of being a slave, is delighted; and he even polishes
the man's shoes. In a confessional mood, he explains: "I

don't understand how to live, what to do," which is the crux of his problem—he cannot cope with life without his mother. The missionary tells him, "you can't stop still at your mother's death" (207)—but the boy has willfully arrested his emotional growth, and inwardly he even resents his physical growth.

After a long conversation with the man, Orvil's disenchantment ensues; for he is disappointed to discover that the ornate religious artifacts in the cabin are just as commercial and mass-produced as secular goods. Orvil had hoped to find something more other-worldly about them. Instead, the altar lamp looked like "one of those swinging bulbs of liquid soap which he loved to turn upside down in public lavatories" (106). In the midst of holy things, Orvil's imagination still focusses on the latrine.

The episode ends disastrously. When Orvil playfully ties up the young headmaster, he retaliates by soundly cuffing him on the head. Orvil retreats without even learning the man's name. Like all his other attempts at escape from Self, this homo-erotic one too has failed. He resolves never to return to the hut.

Orvil's next important encounter, or voyage, is with an older married girl named Aphra, a name which suggests Aphrodite and the lure of heterosexual love. Aphra befriends Orvil and pretends to prefer his innocence to the company of the heavily sexual Charles, Orvil's brother, and his friend Dennis. Like Orvil's mother, Aphra encourages him to play with her jewelry. Orvil is much taken with her, and she is the closest thing to a mother substitute he has found. When a dance is announced for the hotel's guests, he wishes himself a girl, reasoning that as a young boy he cannot ask a grown woman to dance.

In an active gesture of wish fulfillment, he takes the stolen lipstick and in the privacy of his room begins to paint himself. First he paints his lips and then his cheeks. Then he fluffs up his hair. Finally the transvestite urge gives way to his masochistic streak: he undresses and "absentmindedly rouged his nipples until they were like two squashed strawberries. He looked down at them vaguely and then began to rouge all the extremities of his body—the fingertips, the toes, the ear lobes. Next, he made gashes and spots all over his body until he seemed entirely dressed in the crimson marks" (133). Finally, the lonely boy dances in the empty room.

Just as his active search for solace in the church and for homosexual companionship in the woods failed, his projected transvestite longings and hope for friendship with Aphra also come to nothing. Forced to leave the dance by older teenagers, Orvil decides to explore the cottage in the dingle he had seen earlier. Remembering the inadequacy of his knife, he steals a long, strong blade from the hotel dining room to equip himself for the night venture. After he has forced his way inside the cottage, he observes a stained-glass window portraying a saint. He studies the figure and notices "the ivy pushing between the fork of his legs in long green shoots," an image of fertility, potency, and growing manhood. But juxtaposed to the green vine in the groin, Welch gives us another and a more pervading image: there is a large, dead bird decaying on the hearthstone like a sacrifice. The saintly window with its beautiful stained glass and its fertile groin represents idealized manhood which Orvil is never to achieve. His manhood has been sacrificed; and, like the bird it lies cold and dead on the hearth. Hindu tradition has it that birds represent the higher states of being, spirituality or soul. Welch here intuits the boy's despiritualization.

Leaving the cottage, Orvil decides to explore next the adjacent cave, another subconscious return to the womb. But, instead of solace in the cave, he encounters a truly traumatic scene: he stumbles upon his brother Charles, his rival, making love to Aphra. Charles has his lips to the married woman's bare breast, an act especially significant to the boy since it was earlier disclosed that Aphra had been nursing her infant daughter: "He saw Charles' lips and Aphra's breasts swelling and diminishing, like rubber objects first filled with air and then deflated. He saw jets of milk, and fountains pouring down" (146). For Orvil, this scene is equivalent to finding his mother giving suck to someone other than himself.

The next day, when Charles playfully abandons Orvil on the dam in the middle of the lake, Orvil's isolation is symbolic of his prevailing alienation. Aphra's infidelity to her husband and her deceitfulness with Orvil both reinforce the boy's view of the treachery of women. As he watches Aphra leave the hotel by car, his impression of her is that "she looked like a very pretty corpse seen through the beveled-glass window of an expensive coffin" (155). Aphra is now spiritually dead to him, and her vision has become one with that of his mother, who ultimately was unfaithful to him by dying.

After this disillusionment, Orvil leaves the hotel to spend a brief visit in the home of Sir Robert and Lady Winkle. For the most part, this episode marks a digression in the novel; and we almost suspect that Welch is padding the story to make it novel length. But Orvil's aversion to the Winkle's daughter Constance does affirm what has by now been established as his misogyny: "Orvil saw the greenish shadowed valley between her big white breasts. The sight shocked him. He thought of Aphra in the grotto. He saw a hairless white camel in the desert. He was riding on its back, between the humps. They were not really humps but Constance's breasts, or miniature volcanoes with holes at the top, out of which poured clouds of milky-white smoke, and sometimes long, thin, shivering tongues of fire" (108).

To add to Orvil's sexual confusion, Constance's senile grandmother mistakes him for a girl. When corrected, she protests that his hair is so curly that she could not tell the difference. Orvil notices that the old lady's jewels are dirty and dusty, an observation he had made earlier about the Ciro pearls of the hotel employee in black satin. To the young esthete Orvil, who loves jewelry and who spent hours as a child playing with his mother's gems, this recurrent image of soiled jewels connotes the decay of all beauty and values in the world about him since the loss of his Edenic childhood.

When Orvil returns to the hotel from his visit, it is nearly time to resume studies at school. He imagines both family and school authorites to be prowling about him like wild beasts. When he thinks of school, it is in grotesque, Jacobean images: the iron beds are "black enamel skeletons," the blankets are "meat-red," and "everything had a demonish

quality of unreality, a sort of pasteboard attempt at horror."
In this state of mind, he has an apocalyptic vision in which
he sees the river flowing swiftly beneath the old toll bridge:
"It was swollen with the filth of ten thousand cities. Sweat,
excrement, blood, pus poured through the stone arches. The
filth curled into marbled patterns, streaked into horrible
arabesques" (221). Orvil compensates for this vision by
daydreaming of running away, not like a Huck Finn on a
rude raft, but rather like Cleopatra on a baroque barge, "all
golden, with feather fans and music" (223)—a transvestite
dream, hardly an image for any boy aspiring to manhood.

There is, of course, no recourse but to return to school.
After Orvil checks out of the hotel, the novel moves to a
swift climax. In the train, he is brutally victimized by Woods,
an older boy from school who is also making the return trip.
Woods—the name ironically recalls Orvil's unsuccessful
search for succor in the woods—pretends at first that Orvil
is a ravishing milkmaid and he the ravisher. Then, bored,
he takes out a pair of clippers, the very sight of which terri-
fies Orvil. Again we have a sharp, knifelike instrument
brought into play with Orvil's feelings of inadequacy. Woods
holds him down and cuts off Orvil's long eye lashes with
the nail scissors, an act of symbolic emasculation, like
Delilah's undoing of Samson. Orvil becomes hysterical; and,
as he screamed, "he knew that he could not stop, that he had
been working up to this scream all his life" (228).

His brother Ben comes to his rescue, but not until the
lashes have been clipped. Ben hits Woods and then kicks
him directly in the groin, an act of poetic retribution. But
the harm has been done, for Orvil's summer-long search
for self has concluded disasterously. Eye lashes never grow
back, just as Orvil shall never lay claim to masculinity again.
He has run the gamut of self-pity, masochism, sadism,
necrophilia, satanism, exhibitionism, narcissism, and trans-
vestism. Now, totally broken in spirit and symbolically
broken in body, Orvil Pym realizes that nothing will ever
change for him. The summer has been but a brief interlude
away from the brute masculine world to which he can never
lay claim, but in which he is condemned to live out his
life a misfit.

II *Gothicism*

The prevailing mood, of course, is Gothic throughout. *In Youth Is Pleasure* literally drips with Gothic imagery and action. The romantic architecture of the hotel, the empty cottage, the dead bird on the hearth, the mysterious grotto, the torture instruments, and the flaunting of all taboos are part of the fictional landscaping of Gothic novels, just as the innocent voyage culminating in violence, lust, mutilation, and defeat which Orvil undergoes parallels the basic black Gothic plot. In this sense, Orvil Pym is a male version of the Gothic heroine, the maiden in distress who is pursued by vile villains. Like the Gothic heroine, Orvil saw the world as a maze from which he must somehow emerge whole.

The effect is somewhat shrill; at times, the pitch of the short novel rises toward hysteria. Welch most likely saw the appropriation of Gothic machinery as a means of giving an added dimension to his personal story which he had already told before in *Maiden Voyage*. Just as an interpretation of that book reveals a mythic framework, *In Youth Is Pleasure* yields the Gothic. Welch may have been influenced by reading Matthew Lewis, Mrs. Radcliffe, or any number of Gothic writers; but Jane Austen's *Northanger Abbey* could have given him the notion of inflicting Gothic machinery upon his confessional novel. (We know from his *Journals* that he was a Jane Austenite.) Austen, however, used the Gothic trappings only to satirize them; Welch, on the other hand, drags them in in dead earnest, like so many of Marley's chains. The result is heavy-handed, especially in so short a novel. *In Youth Is Pleasure,* while displaying novelistic form and control and a concision far more admirably than that exhibited in *Maiden Voyage,* must ultimately be consigned to a place somewhat below that accorded Welch's first and third novels.

CHAPTER 4

The Early Stories:
Brave and Cruel

FOR some novelists the writing of short stories is purely a diversion, and the results are works which are of secondary importance. Such is not the case with Denton Welch, for his stories represent a significant portion of his work and the execution of them consumed a significant portion of his energies. Eric Oliver has related how Welch abandoned work on his unfinished masterpiece, *A Voice Through a Cloud* for the expressed purpose of writing stories which eventually appeared in *Brave and Cruel* and which testify not so much to his economic need as to the seriousness with which he approached his shorter pieces.[1] His stories appeared individually in *Horizon, English Story, New Writing, Cornhill,* and elsewhere; and his letters reveal that publisher Hamish Hamilton requested as early as 1944 a book of Welch's stories.

Nevertheless, *Brave and Cruel,* the first of his two story collections, ironically was not published until several days after his death in 1948. Welch personally had selected the contents from among all his stories written between 1943 and 1947, and the quality was consistently high. *A Last Sheaf,* the posthumous collection published in 1951 and edited by Eric Oliver, contains three stories Welch wrote in the last year of his life after *Brave and Cruel* had gone to press ("The Hateful Word," "The Diamond Badge," and "A Picture in the Snow"), plus eight others that Welch had chosen not to include in *Brave and Cruel.* His critical acumen concerning his own work appears correct; for, of the stories which remained unpublished at the time of his death, only "The Hateful Word" and perhaps "The Diamond Badge" are as successful as the best pieces in the first collection.

Several stories in *Brave and Cruel*—"The Fire in the Wood," "At Sea," "The Coffin on the Hill," and his best-known story, "When I Was Thirteen"—must be counted among Welch's most remarkable achievements. Though it is usually the novels *Maiden Voyage* and *A Voice Through a Cloud* for which Welch is remembered, when he is remembered at all, his stories are in some ways more satisfying and more artistically successful. Certainly "The Fire in the Wood" and "The Hateful Word" are much better examples of the short story than any of his novels is of the novel. "The Fire in the Wood," in fact, is a perfectly realized example of its genre which could not be said of any one of Welch's novels, however singularly interesting it may be. His exercise of greater control and selectivity when writing in the shorter form is a contributing factor to the power and economy of *In Youth Is Pleasure*, his shortest novel; and its technique bears testimony to his study of short-story craft. The most consciously formed of his novels, *In Youth Is Pleasure* is at least technically his best; and it is primarily the frankness of its subject matter which has caused the book to be overly denigrated by critics. Indeed, Jocelyn Brooke, who has written at length on two occasions about Welch's novels, has confessed that for him the book's "frequent descriptions of masturbation fantasies become slightly embarrassing."[2]

The stories of *Brave and Cruel* are of widely varying kinds. Some, such as "Narcissus Bay" and "Leaves from a Young Person's Notebook," are mere sketches. Others—"The Trout Stream" and "The Fire in the Wood"—are well-structured stories approaching novella length. "Brave and Cruel," the title piece, is a short novel. The other five stories in the collection are of conventional length. For the most part, the themes of the stories are the concerns of all of Welch's writings: youth's vulnerablility and growing awareness of mortality; the body's betrayal of the spirit; the impossibility of reciprocal love; alienation and instability; isolation and personal dissociation. The book bears evidence for the first time of Welch's existentialist thinking. His usual

strong misogynistic feelings are scarcely evident, except in
"The Barn" and in "The Fire in the Wood." In the latter
story Welch employs what Stanley Edgar Hyman has called
The Albertine Strategy; like Proust, Welch narrates the
latter story from a woman's point of view. The feminine
disguise may have been assumed for reasons of prudence,
since the story recalls a love affair, but what is important
is that Welch succeeds in projecting the persona, thereby
making a breakthrough from his usual first-person singular
confessional narratives.

Other currents running throughout the book include
strong anti-American feelings expressed in several stories
and a graphic statement in "The Trout Stream" about the
sterility of materialism—an unusual development for a writer so personally preoccupied with collecting china, silver,
antiques, and objets d'art. A number of the tales also are concerned with voyages, among them the opening story, "The
Coffin on the Hill," which in reality is about one boy's voyage
from childhood innocence to painful awareness of mortality.
The story is told in highly symbolic terms and is worth examining in detail as a model for Welch's method in the shorter
genre.

I   *"The Coffin on the Hill"*

The protagonist's voyage occurs at Eastertime, the traditional time of rebirth and man's remembrance of God's
promise of life after death. Welch has encapsuled the entire
story in symbolic terms in the first sentence: "Perhaps I was
eight when my parents took me at Easter time up the river
in a house-boat."[3] To the boy, the parents represent security;
the river is the river of life, the life force; the houseboat,
the ark, the vessel of the spirit afloat on the river of life. Together, the boy and his parents set out to "explore the canals
and waterways," life in its various aspects.

Early in the story there is a foreshadowing of the knowledge
that the young narrator is later to attain: the boat's cook
and coolie tease the boy by giving a superstitious explanation
for the river's current; they tell him that, if he fell overboard,
the drowned people below would pull him down and keep

him under until he, too, drowned. The boy is shaken by the story; he carries with him terrible visions:

arms like water-weeds or octopus tentacles stretched up to grasp my kicking legs, dragging me down, not demonishly, but with a horrible, greedy sort of love, as though they wanted to keep me and gloat on me forever. I thought of the dead faces: The eyes, the nose, the mouth eaten away by fishes. But they were still able to weep from the holes where their eyes had been, and cries locked in bubbles escaped from the shapeless mouths. (7)

Later, when the boy returns to his cabin, he curls up in a corner and feels "like a mole or some other perfectly happy, blind animal, burrowing deeper and deeper, coming at last to its true home" (10). Upset by the frightening story, he assumes the prenatal position. His burrowing sensation is an expression of the desire to return to the womb, to recapture the one perfect state of innocence before man is born to worldly knowledge.

When his mother discovers him in this withdrawn state, she puts him in bed beside the curious doll he insists on keeping despite his advanced age of eight years and his being a boy. The doll, of course, is an outward manifestation of his inner desire to remain in the dependent and innocent state of childhood; the doll bears the curious name of Lymph Est. (Significantly, in former times, anyone inclined toward sleepiness or sluggishness was said to possess too much lymph in his system.) Neither masculine nor feminine, Lymph Est appears totally sexless—a symbol of preadolescent selfhood, that state of happiness before sex raises its head in puberty. The child narrator admits that he frequently talked to the doll because of his need for an audience, for his loneliness is extreme.

The morning after hearing the dreadful tale the boy awakes to find "long grasses poking through the port hole." Obviously, the young hero has arrived at a region of fecund maturity. Ashore, he visits an ancient monastery, symbol of all that is mysterious to him as a Protestant. He marvels at the monks with their shaven heads, black robes, and clacking wooden rosaries. Even the monks' odor emphasizes their strangeness, possessing "a curious smell both animal and aromatic" (12), one which fills the boy with uneasiness.

Leaving the monks, the family drifts farther down the river. The boy fears that logs (obstacles in his path) will end the voyage by wrecking the boat, but somehow the boat always proceeds smoothly. The next stop is for a picnic on a grassy knoll. To reach the top of the ridge they must climb upward through broken terraces and tangled bushes—a climb suggestive of man's uphill journey through the thickets of life. At the end of the climb, the boy and his family encounter a graveyard, as do all at the end of life's journey. There, amidst thousands of hidden skeletons, the family has its picnic. In a gesture honoring his increased maturity, the boy is allowed coffee in his milk.

The boy runs off to explore after eating, and what he finds is a gaping, open grave. He can see a coffin inside, and even the remains of a piece of cloth through a crack in the rotten wood. This sight jolts his eight-year-old mind; he understands for the first time man's fate. His journey down the river and his climb up the hill have terminated in terrible knowledge, knowledge of the mortality of the flesh which man is powerless against: "The imprisoned concealed smell of the monks had been bad, but there was a worse, more evil smell here—a smell that was forcing me to know what happened in the end. Rotting wood and cloth and human bone were changed now. They were dead" (16).

From this epiphany he returns to the place he had left his parents, only to discover they are no longer there. He panics, fearing desertion in his blackest hour; and his insecurity has now reached its apogee. When he finally finds his mother, she is meditating in the tomb garden. He would like to tell her what he has seen and acknowledged, but he knows he cannot. Her attitude has always been that one does not discuss such matters, and now he especially feels the gulf between them, just as he perceives the transitory nature of her very existence: "She seemed the very opposite of all that the coffin held, but this only made my confusion worse, for I knew that she would come to it at last; and that knowledge was unbearable" (17).

The next morning marks the family's return to the city, a voyage to the center of civilization. Lying in his bunk, the boy contemplates both the actual shroud he saw in the coffin and the legendary tale of the drowned people in the river. In a symbolic gesture, he throws the doll Lymph Est out the porthole: "I saw Lymph Est's squat limbs, silk face, whorish black eyes, and scarlet mouth all framed in the mud-green water. No dead men dragged it down. The kapok stuffing kept it floating perfectly. Lymph Est was unmolested and serene and doomed" (18-19).

The doll at this point is a surrogate for the boy—apparently unharmed, yet already marked for destruction. And, as symbol of the boy's innocence, it is cast off and sacrificed to knowledge. The boat that the boy floats in is but a larger version of the coffin in which he knows he will someday rest. At eight years of age, the pall of the grave has fallen across his life; and he will never again be the same.

II *"The Barn"*

A more simple story is "The Barn." As in "The Coffin on the Hill," the tale is narrated by a lonely boy with great feelings of inadequacy; and he is obviously the fictional counterpart of the author as a child. The story opens with a scene of physical failure in which the youth is unable to skid a bicycle correctly, an act of mechanical failure which possibly is fraught with Freudian implications. The writing here is reminiscent of *In Youth Is Pleasure*, charged as it is with strongly misogynistic feelings. The narrator's older brother taunts him, saying he prefers the company of old ladies to that of boys; but the narrator actually hates women. When Mrs. Singleton accidentally appears before the boy in disarray, he registers disgust rather than boyish curiosity: "The next moment she appeared before me in all the glory of soiled and elaborate corsets, which reached from her bosom to her pale grey thighs. She wore no stockings, and the suspenders dangled uselessly against her heavy blue-veined legs. Her hair was like a nest made by some very slovenly rook"(22).

The boy flees to the empty barn, where he solitarily acts out imaginary games. First, he pretends he is a monkey, swinging from a beam; then he is a slave, sweating and naked; and, finally, he is a prisoner, stripped by the hangman. He looks at the whiteness of his skin and wistfully thinks "of the men I had seen, with tufts of strong hair on their chests and under their arms. It was ugly and beautiful at once " (23). The boy wants desperately to be grown up and strong. In his subliminal fantasies, he is projecting his image of ideal companionship and of the man he should like to become.

Into this unhappy situation the author casts a tramp, who comes to the house and asks for a night's shelter in the barn. The boy resolves to visit the barn in the middle of the night under the pretense of making the man more comfortable. Actually, he is voyaging out in search of companionship and his image of idealized manhood. When he tries to evoke a spirit of comraderie between them by telling the tramp he'd also like to rough it, the man tells him he is too soft; and the boy is again reminded of his physical inadequacies. Hurt, he tells the tramp about the exercises he does every day in the barn, his preparations for manhood. But he is again mocked.

Only when they fall asleep together are they equals: during the night, the tramp instinctively puts his arm around the boy; they are in sleep brothers at last. But after breakfast—a small communion they share, like Maurice's walk on the beach with Dr. Farley in *A Voice Through a Cloud*—the man takes to the road and again rejects him. The boy is left as lonely as before, waiting out his childhood. A corollary concern of the story is the narrator's comparison between the tramp and Mrs. Singleton. The former's flesh is hard and desirable; the latter's repulsive; and the reader may deduce that the story's protagonist is on his way to becoming a homosexual.

III   *"Narcissus Bay"*

No doubt the most elusive story in the collection is "Narcissus Bay." In his book-length study of decadent literature, C. E. M. Joad attempted to explicate the story, and concluded that it "was about nothing at all." He then stated that Welch's story is typical of many works of decadence—works which are based on the assumption that "any experience is significant and worthy of record, irrespective of the quality of the experience or the nature of the 'object' of which it is an experience."[4] Although the point of "Narcissus Bay" *is* evasive, a careful reading of the story does reveal it to be carefully constructed by its author.

The story begins with a violent scene which the young narrator observes: four men and a woman come down from the mountain, and two of the men have their hands bound behind them. Their chests are naked, thick ropes are cruelly tied around their necks. The woman obviously has been the victim of some attack by the two, who are now on their way to punishment. As for the woman, "Her dust black hair was torn down over her face and shoulders. Blood oozed from cuts on her scalp; a patch of oiled paper had been stuck over one gash, and her lips were swollen and bruised."

After observing this procession, the boy spends the remainder of the day in the company of playmates. Quotidian event follows quotidian event in a seemingly senseless and artless pattern. Yet the violence of the initial scene exerts itself and pervades the rest of the day. Two young girls he encounters on the beach are cruel to their fat Belgian governess, whom they have "by a rope." The boy Adam is cruel to young Derek; he not only tells him to eat dead flowers, and to drink slimy green water, he also fills him full of traumatic tales. The narrator, in turn, is subtly cruel to Adam by swimming playfully while the boy is incapacitated. The story, then, is a chain or "rope" of incidents all leading back to the memory of the original scene of cruelty. The civilized children are portrayed as being as cruel and, in their quiet way, as violent as the native men who were brought down from the woods for punishment.

Above the action of the story, located on the mountain over them all, sits the site of a shrine. Symbolic of man's higher impulses (religion), the shrine is nevertheless an "utterly still, deserted place" where baked mud gods are "gazing down, unmoving, caught in a trance, just watching everything, holding up their fingers, flashing their eyes and teeth forever" (36). The gods, then, are silent and immoveable—if they exist they are in all probability cruel themselves. Welch seems to be saying that man preys on those weaker than himself, and abases himself before those stronger. All of mankind is depraved, and the procession of men roped together which initiated the story is a potent symbol for our human bondage to evil; the barren altar which concludes the story signifies the absence of any order in the universe save superstition and depravity. We see in the pool of Narcissus Bay our own reflections.

By extension the story also makes a case for the inequality of justice. The children of the well-to-do and presumably the well-to-do themselves, can escape retribution, but the uneducated and the underprivileged must pay for their abuses.

IV *"At Sea"*

"My mother is young and pretty, most people's mothers look old and ugly," thinks the boy Robert at the outset of "At Sea," another story of a journey and a transformation. As with most of Welch's youthful protagonists and their mothers, Robert is a Mama's Boy and his mother is a strong Christian Scientist. Unlike "The Coffin on the Hill," to which this story is related in theme and characterization, in "At Sea" the special nature of the mother-son relationship is dramatized by their being on an ocean voyage together and without the boy's father.

Early in the story Robert and his mother quarrel, and he goes off to brood. In a symbolic act, he writes a long letter on the ship's notepaper—only to discover there is no one in the world to whom he can address it; and his written outburst of self-expression is discarded unaddressed. Besides his mother, he feels utterly alone. Robert's world is an extremely narrow one—one so confined that he even sees the sea in domestic terms. The Atlantic appears to him to be "an endless carpet, bulging and yielding, because of the draught along the floor boards beneath it" (48). Later, Welch introduces the princess and her dog as doppelgangers for Robert's mother and himself. The dog on the chain is a symbolic figure of Robert and his ties to his mother. When the Princess confesses that she and her dog must be separated when the ship reaches Southampton, we are given a foreshadowing of Robert's fate.

The story progresses to a shipboard cocktail party, where his mother dances with a Mr. Barron. Robert's Oedipal jealousy becomes so great that he loses all control of himself and urinates in his pants. Mr. Barron's function in the story however, is far greater than merely to provoke Robert's jealousy: he is described as managing "to look like a skeleton" (45) and later is said to smile "like a dead man" (49). For his name, Barron, we should read "barren" or "Charon —for he is a Charon figure, the mythological personification of Death that has come to claim Robert's mother.[5] The dance Mr. Barron and Robert's mother perform at the party is the dance of death, a *valse triste*; and it is no accident that the recording which the gramophone insistently plays is titled, "My Cutie's Due at Two-to-Two on a Big Choo-Choo," emphasizing her impending deathly appointment. The ship then becomes Charon's boat as he claims her and guides her across the River Styx.

Robert's mother does not die that evening, but the boy has acquired the knowledge that she shall die. At the story's conclusion, she sits looking "lost, unhappy, and unwell" (53); and her appearance forms a striking contrast to Welch's initial description of her. Robert realizes that she can do nothing to save herself and that his temporary loss of her at the party has been merely a trial enactment of the permanent physical loss which is to come. When she dies, her death will be for him the worst kind of trauma; and he will spend his days quite "at sea"—alone—which gives ironic point to the title Welch chose.

Both "At Sea" and "The Coffin on the Hill" deal with childhood journeys by water to terrible knowledge or mortality. And in their portraits of American tourists, both reveal strong anti-American feelings on the part of the author. The stories differ greatly, however, in their emotional quality. In "The Coffin on the Hill," the youthful protagonist voyages into knowledge of mortality; but it is a generalization about the nature of human kind that he achieves. In "At Sea," however, it is the particularization of death's impending claim upon his own mother that is so utterly shattering and immediate.

V *"When I Was Thirteen"*

Welch's best-known story, "When I Was Thirteen,"[6] is concerned with the acquisition of another kind of experiential knowledge, one culminating not in painful awareness of the norm of mortality but of abnormal sexuality. The story explores the delicate distinctions of the youthful psyche and the labyrinthine regions of the human soul, and it does so with candor and skill.

The setting is a ski resort in Switzerland, and the time is during Christmas holidays. The narrator's point of view and the descriptions of the snowy afternoons establish the young protagonist's innocence and freshness of outlook. When he and Archer sit reading on the hotel's sun terrace, he has to ask the older boy what an "illegitimate child" is, a term he has just read. When Archer explains, the boy refuses to believe him: "I still believed that it was quite impossible to have a child unless one was married. The very fact of being married produced the child. I had a vague idea that some particularly reckless people attempted, without being married, to have children in places called 'night clubs,' but they were always unsuccessful, and this made them drink, and plunge into the most hectic gaiety" (60).

Against this wide-eyed innocence, Archer is placed as a foil: while the younger boy reads the classics, Archer reads sex adventures. Archer represents everything the narrator is not. His very name connotes an athletic temperament, while the narrator is delicate and artistic. Yet they share a common sense of exclusion. Just as the narrator is too young to ski with his older brother's friends, so Archer for some unstated reason is not invited to join the popular crowd. Perhaps out of loneliness as much as kindness he befriends the younger boy, and he treats him as he would an adult, which the boy desperately needs. Their friendship becomes something quite beautiful, and Archer becomes to the thirteen-year-old boy a hero, even a savior. When Archer carries the skis of both boys, "he looked like a very tough Jesus carrying two crosses" (62).

Their relationship commences a series of initiations for the narrator. Leaving the sensual and psychic indulgences of hot chocolate and cake, he acquires an adult's awareness of cigarettes, rum, and finally crème de menthe, on which he gets drunk. But, while Archer is obviously a sensual person (and even employs the boy to scrub his bare back), there are no sexual initiations. Despite the purity of their relationship, the narrator's brother ultimately interprets their idyl in Archer's cabin as a homosexual tryst. He accuses the younger boy of being a "Bastard, Devil, Harlot, Sod!" The sad truth was that the only one of those words the boy had even heard before was "Devil." The boy had experienced the small initiations but not the sexual one of which he was falsely and violently accused. And, sadly, his one link with the adult world has now been broken; he must regress to a state of limbo once again. But such setbacks ultimately make a boy a man.

Just as the reader is kept from knowing enough about the true character of Henry James's Peter Quint in *The Turn of the Screw* to determine the degree of corruption it would be possible for him to instill in the seemingly innocent young Miles, so it is with Welch's Archer. Why the older brother's crowd avoided him, we are never told; we simply know that "they were not at the same college, but they had met and evidently had not agreed with each other." Later, when asked about Archer, the older brother simply states, "He's not very much liked; although he's a very good swimmer." As he gave this reply, the brother is said to have "held his lips in a very firm, almost pursed, line which was most damaging to Archer" (56).

At the story's conclusion, the reader may have reason to conjecture that the cause for the older brother's dislike of Archer was a knowledge of some tainted aspect of Archer's personality. Specifically, if Archer were known at school to be a homosexual, we would have the cause for the brother's outburst and concern at the story's conclusion; and the homoerotic nuances of Archer's behaviour would have been deliberate. But, since we are never told, the brother's violent reaction to seeing Archer and his brother together could be a manifestation of his own hidden sexual predilections; and, being homosexual by inclination himself, he could well have read homosexuality into the innocent friendship of the pair.

Or more damning, he could secretly have been attracted to Archer and therefore jealous of his younger brother.

The point remains that the relationship had been above reproach until the advent of the older brother on the scene. As Basil Davenport has written, the story "delicately suggests how the physical intimacy of the holiday trembles on the verge of the morbid—or perhaps better is the raw material from which the morbid can arise—and yet would have remained perfectly clean and healthy if the situation had not been precipitated by suspicion."[7] Once the suspicion is voiced, however, the young boy must ultimately question not only his very nature but also Archer's motivations. The snow has been dirtied, and he will never see the world through the same clear eyes that he did when thirteen. He will recall the holiday with shame. His innocence is corrupted by the older brother's imaginings, by his sick turning of the screw.

VI *"The Judas Tree"*

More suspect is the motivation behind the attempt at friendship for a young art student that is evinced by a retired schoolmaster in "The Judas Tree." When the reader is first introduced to the man, he is carrying a posy, a reminder of Oscar Wilde's familiar prop. Welch portrays the schoolmaster as a Wilde figure, a dilettante and a dandy, probably manic and at least latently homosexual. The story recalls James Joyce's early tale, "An Encounter," in which the youthful protagonist confronts a corrupted adult. Just as the pervert in "An Encounter" suggests what men find in place of God when they are unable to attain Joyce's "Pigeon House"—the source of power and light—so the schoolmaster is seized with an obsession more sexual than theological, for his obsession is to possess a picture of the biblical Judas hanged. All his life he has collected paintings of Judas, but all are Last Suppers or betrayal scenes. Since he has never found one of Judas on the tree, paid out and fulfilled, he implores the young artist to paint such a picture to end his search.

In his obsession with Judas pictures, the schoolmaster has chosen a fetish which serves to symbolize his own parapathy. The red hair with which Judas traditionally is endowed by painters and the mythical red blossoms of the Judas tree are the color of blood and sensuality. The schoolmaster's identification with Judas is, in all probability, due to his own feelings of guilt, that are caused by his homosexual nature which has had to be sublimated because of his profession. To see Judas hanged would be to work out his own guilt in transference. Furthermore, the Judas pictures, as they would be seen in Stekelian psychology, are fetishes which safeguard the schoolmaster against sin and protect him against women while, at the same time, providing him with a much-needed substitute pleasure.[8]

We witness his excitement and intensity when making the request for the painting: "Could you paint me a picture of Judas hanging dead from the Judas tree, with the beautiful rose-red flowers all around him? You could do the flowers very large, and I want Judas really dead. His tongue must be hanging out, black and swollen. It would make a wonderful picture, and I've been trying to get it painted for years" (78). The schoolmaster not only extracts from the boy a promise to do the painting, but also a commitment to begin visiting regularly for voice lessons.

But the boy does neither; he avoids the man; and, at the story's conclusion, when he accidentally encounters the schoolmaster, the student suddenly perceives the old man's loneliness. He is a schoolmaster with no school, no students to befriend or bully. The boy suddenly wishes to make up for his neglect, but the schoolmaster—hurt—rejects him totally. The art student himself has become a Judas figure in betraying the man's friendship and intentions.

"The Judas Tree" is a comment on the fragility of human relationships. As in "When I Was Thirteen," Welch is saying that human motivation is many times unfathomable and that we are too quick to judge one another unfairly. And, just as the boy is put off by the schoolmaster's intensity, so too is the schoolmaster too quick to let his false pride stand between him and a valued companion. The story also contrasts the loneliness of old age with the gaiety of youth, but it is significant that the youth perceives the sorrow that is the lot of the aged and realizes that such sorrow will also be his inheritance. In this regard, "The Judas Tree" is related thematically to the other stories of knowledge painfully acquired, "The Coffin on the Hill" and "At Sea."

VII *"The Trout Stream"*

The central character in "The Trout Stream"—a long story in three parts—is Mr. Mellon, who is fabulously wealthy but physically incapacitated. His paralysis from the waist down, like that of Lawrence's Sir Clifford in *Lady Chatterley's Lover,* is symbolic of the emotional paralysis of his class of men in the world today; and the story is Welch's protest against the vacuity of materialism. As is appropriate for such a theme, the story's opening image is one of sterility, for the narrator's hotel room overlooks "the fossilized trees in the gardens of the Natural History Museum" (86). All that was natural and beautiful is now arrested and dormant. In Part I, the narrator relates his visit to Mr. Mellon, whose name ironically suggests that which is fruitful, the ripe, the sweet life, and also that of a famous multi-millionaire American family. The narrator's first impression is that everything of Mr. Mellon's estate is "hard and ugly and beautifully kept" (88). The boy possesses an exquisite curiosity; and, after thoroughly investigating the house, he sadly concludes that "all Mr. Mellon's possessions looked as if no one had ever wanted to use them or enjoy them" (93).

Welch heaps images of deadness one after another to convey the total barrenness of Mellon's existence. An image central to the story is that of the beautiful ivory carving of a beggar which the boy examines. On close examination, he discerns that the beggar is covered with rats; the rats are an image of the sickness which pervades the world and prevails even in the presence of great richness and beauty. Earlier in the story, while traveling by train to Mr. Mellon's house, the narrator's mother revealed her first traces of the sickness which was soon to kill her; and Mr. Mellon himself is quite infirm. The carved beggar which is covered by rats represents symbolically their illnesses as well.

During the first of three visits to Mr. Mellon, the young narrator meets Phyllis Slade, the daughter of Mr. Mellon's housekeeper. Phyllis is a cold, unattractive, and tough type

whose pet horse is a symbol of her masculinity. Part II commences some six years after the boy's first visit in Part I.
During this time his mother has died and Mrs. Slade and
Phyllis have won Mr. Mellon's affections, and the girl is to
be officially adopted by him. Mr. Mellon now occupies a
new house, one even more sterile than the last, which the
narrator calls "a gigantic lavatory" (112). One feature of the
new estate is a trout stream in which the fish are confined
within an underwater grating so that they cannot escape.
The trout stream as a symbol is integral to parts II and III,
just as the ivory beggar is in Part I. The infested beggar
and the entrapped trout reinforce Welch's meaning.

Mr. Mellon's money can buy a way to confine fish to his
estate, but in no way can he buy or confine the human heart
or overcome the individual will. By Part III, Phyllis has
eloped with Mr. Mellon's chauffeur Bob, and Mrs. Slade
has drowned herself in the trout steam. Mr. Mellon, who
elevated Mrs. Slade and lavished money and praise on the
stupid Phyllis and Bob, is abandoned by all three. One of the
final images of the story is the blankness of the windows
of Mr. Mellon's house, which are great empty eyes looking
on nothing.

VIII *"Leaves from a Young Person's Notebook"*

"Leaves From a Young Person's Notebook" is not a story
so much as a sketch which anticipates Welch's novel, *A
Voice Through A Cloud*. "Leaves" is the brief narrative of a
sick boy who lives in limbo between several worlds—the
adult world and childhood, the world of the well and the
very sick. The scene he views from his sickroom window is
a microcosm of the cold macrocosm beyond: "The isolated
cast-iron lamp-posts and seats on this esplanade were pierc-
ingly sad. In my curious state of health, it was very easy for
men to see them as lonely, tortured creatures rooted and
anchored just out of shouting distance of one another. The
loneliness of that never-ending expanse of leathery sea was
horribly accentuated by those florid shapes in brittle cast-
iron" (119).

Because of the boy's confused sense of identity, he revels
in all discrepancies between appearance and reality, be-

tween one state and another: he relishes his suntan because
it gives him the appearance of health; he alters an obscene
drawing on a public wall until the pictured woman is transformed into a madonna; and nothing is what it appears to be,
and everything is nothing. The boy makes a clandestine
journey into town in search of meaning in life—another
voyage in search of self in Welch's stories; for he feels he
can gain insight by momentarily leaving his sickbed. But,
before the night is over, he is only more confused; and, on
his return, he wishes to return symbolically to the womb
and imagines he is "a baby Kangaroo in Sister Howe's
pouch."

Compared to the stories that precede it, "Leaves from a
Young Person's Notebook" is an inferior example of the
story teller's art; It lacks tension, plot, and character development. But it presents an arresting if static existential
statement of alienation and instability which Welch was to
expand on and elevate to art in a fully developed portrait
in his last novel.

IX *"Brave and Cruel"*

Appearance versus reality is also a major theme of "Brave
and Cruel," the short novel, or long story, which gives the
collection its title and one which Edith Sitwell hailed as
"extraordinary."[9] The narrator, a successful writer named
Dave, recalls the misadventures of a young man who called
himself Micki Beaumont. From the outset, Micki is obviously a braggart and a chronic liar; and the story relates
how he progressively duped Julia Bellingly, an aging romantic; Katherine Warde, an eligible maiden; and Mrs.
Warde, Katherine's mother. The narrator, however, is
never duped by the boy's prevarications; and his oil portrait of Micki shocks the young imposter early in the story.
Looking at Dave's portrait of himself is an enforced confrontation with reality for Micki—at the reality that is in
any form alien to him.

Central to the short novel is the legend of the blackamoor
who searched everywhere for some magic potion to turn
himself white. Micki, symbolically, is very swarthy and is
always washing his skin. He is a chronic malcontent who

devotes his life to attempting to be what he is not. At first
the narrator's (and the reader's) attitude toward Micki is one
of ridicule; but the story explores the dangers beneath the
surface of the ridiculous, as when no one exposes the boy
and he proceeds in his plans to marry Katherine, a wedding
no one believed could take place. By allowing the imposter to live his lie without interfering, the bystanders almost
permit the girl to be trapped in an impossible marriage.
Just as Micki caused the unreal to seem real, the real had
suddenly become unreal. There clearly are times for human
responsibility, Welch is saying, times when interference
is justified, and this instance is one.

Images of Micki in his various guises dominate the short
novel, for the portrait of him executed by the narrator later
is contrasted with official police photographs which the investigating officer carries. "An indescribable air of degrad-
ation hung about him in each picture," Dave relates. "To
look at the horrible card made one feel ashamed. No one
should ever be seen in that state, I thought" (183). Human
dignity has been sacrificed, and Micki is ultimately a pathetic figure. Whereas the reader's attitude toward him had
been one of ridicule, Micki is revealed at the conclusion to
be one of two sons of a poor farmer who has vainly attempted to transcend his poverty and his ordinariness. In confronting and defying the class structure of his country, he
has resorted to mendacity and self-delusion. He presented
himself as a figure both "brave and cruel" but in reality he
was neither.

Because of a subtle twist of storytelling, the narrator,
Dave, appears ignoble to the reader because of his snobbish-
ness and class consciousness—his beliefs that people should
"stay in their appointed places" (193). In many ways, Dave
seems less admirable than Micki, who is hunted down by
the law for his delusions while people like Dave remain free
to practice subtler social schemes. Welch gives the story yet
a final twist when he presents a climactic view of Micki who,
free again, has risen like the phoenix from the ashes of his
affair with Katherine. Micki is glimpsed on a bus, well-
dressed and in apparent good circumstances, presumably in
the midst of more prevarication and chicanery. Something

in Micki's absolutely driven personality that won't admit
defeat makes the reader hope that Micki will succeed and
achieve to some degree the status that is so important to
him.

"Brave and Cruel" is good reading, for it contains in
Katherine, Micki, and Mrs. Bellingly some of Denton
Welch's best-delineated characters. And Welch also displays
one side of his talent sometimes absent in stories such as
"Narcissus Bay" and "Leaves from a Young Person's Notebook"—his acute sense of humor. With apparent delight he
relates Julia Bellingly's bawdy little stories (177, 205), jokes
which have not lost a whit of their wit since they were published some twenty years before. The short novel also shows
Welch at the height of his descriptive powers, as when he
comments on Julia: "The blue eyes were two smoky peb-
bles, washed up by the cold sea, and the mouth had set into
a dark crimson line, finishing in sharp little down-curving
fishhooks" (152).

But the untoward length of the story is not entirely justified by its content. Despite its apparent excellences,
"Brave and Cruel" is not the capstone of the collection.
Those laurels are reserved for "The Fire in the Wood," the
final story in the volume.

X   *"The Fire in the Wood"*

Nowhere in his writings did Denton Welch succeed more
totally than in "The Fire in the Wood," a story in which he
fuses symbol and theme, character and act, into a perfect
whole. Excellent as the parts of each of his three novels may
be, as totals they are less than satisfactory because they are
picaresque and discursive. "The Fire in the Wood," on the
other hand, moves from opening to closing in a swift and
deft manner. The story immediately proclaims its superiority
to those which precede it by the assured quality of its style:
"On the edge of a pine wood in Hampshire there is a little
concrete box which dates from the time when such architecture
was still fashionable and rare. It looks a little forlorn and
posturing now, but inside it is comfortable enough . . ."
(207).

The house is cement, one of the most impenetrable of materials; and its occupant, a young virgin appropriately named Mary, lives her days in complete indifference to a world which never penetrates her consciousness. A painter, Mary lives totally in the imagination. As a child, she was aloof from all her playmates; and even now the needlework pictures she sews are fantasies, the dragons she stitches pretty and unreal. In Mary's life, there are no real or metaphorical dragons to slay; and even the forest in which her house sets is artificial, a man-made retreat.

Into this life comes a woodsman named Jim, whose job it is to clear the forest—or, in allegorical terms, to cut down the barricade Mary has erected between herself and reality. Jim is a natural force and an intrusion, yet she manages to interpret him in unreal, storybook terms. First she imagines him to be some earth god: "His whole body was so covered with little smears of mud and charcoal, little bits of moss, twig and leaf, that she found it easy to imagine him rising out of the ground itself" (208). Later, she translates him into some Oriental god: his belt clasp winks and glints "like some great eye or jewel in his stomach" (215). Her other visions of him include Sinbad, Gulliver, Robin Hood, even Rip Van Winkle—anything but a real man with real flesh and blood.

The fire which Jim builds in the woods is a symbol of the love which he kindles in Mary. She becomes emotionally involved for the first time, but here is a romantic involvement only. When Jim's mother accompanies him to his job, she tells Mary tales about an epileptic daughter, an abnormal grandchild, and an injured mother-in-law. When these stories of painful reality intrude upon Mary's dreamworld, she runs away; but she finds no escape from reality. The local idiot child who is ubiquitous throughout the story (like Hawthorne's little Pearl in *The Scarlet Letter*) ultimately serves as the bearer of symbolic reality. After Mary has discovered that Jim is not a mythic figure but a man with one's problems—the husband of a bad woman and the father of an abnormal child—the idiot child places a maimed, bloody bird at Mary's head where she will discover it on regaining consciousness. The moment Mary opens her eyes, she will gaze on brute reality: the forest has been cleared, and she must see life as it is lived.

Her neighbor's pronouncement, "It's no good! It doesn't do to love anything; if one does, the thing is sure to be destroyed"(211) has been Mary's philosophy too. She has kept her distance from the world for fear of being burned, but the world ultimately came to her with its fires. Mary must pay for her total disengagement and lack of human involvement, and the price she pays is a deep love for Jim which shall remain forever unrequited.

"The Fire in the Wood" is the most Laurentian of Welch's stories, dealing as it does with the encounter of a repressed female and a natural man, as well as championing the instinctive rather than the intellectual forces. Throughout both of Welch's collections of stories, we discern affinities for Lawrence's fiction—as in the Sir Clifford figure of Mr. Mellon, in the Lady Chatterly figure of Phyllis Slade who runs away with the chauffeur-masseur, and in Welch's Laurentian hatred for industrialization.[10]

"The Fire in the Wood" is the only story in the collection in which the sympathetic protagonist is a female and not a sensitive male. Whether or not the reader interprets Mary as another of Welch's personal personae, and the story one of homosexuality rather than heterosexuality, is ultimately beside the point.[11] The story succeeds on both levels and is an impressive and somewhat inevitable conclusion to the collection. Inevitable because *Brave and Cruel* is a book which presents a chronological progression of protagonists who are the author's personae. From stories like "The Coffin on the Hill," "The Barn," and "At Sea"—in which Welch's fictional counterpart is a very young child—we move into adolescence with "When I Was Thirteen" and "The Judas Tree." Then "Leaves from a Young Person's Notebook" presents the artist as a young man. The narrator of "Brave and Cruel" is a young adult of some accomplishment. And, finally, "The Fire in the Wood" presents a mature individual quite set in a pattern of behavior who encounters for the first time an overwhelming emotion.

Whether the protagonist is called Robert, Dave, Denton, or even Mary, we are tracing the growth of the same sensibility. If we choose to read the volume as a kind of autobiography, it would serve as a parallel to Virginia Woolf's fictional homage to Vita Sackville-West, *Orlando,* in which the protagonist literally changes sex during the course of the action, a comment on the bisexuality present in us all. But to read *Brave and Cruel* only in such a manner ultimately would be to distort the author's intention. The parts were offered as individual stories, and as such several of them succeed as well as anything Denton Welch was to write. The book deserves to be reprinted and made available again.

CHAPTER 5

A Voice Through A Cloud

I *Rebirth Through Agony*

WELCH'S valedictory novel recounts yet another voyage, an odyssey from health to illness to partial recovery; and it explores along the way various stages in the liberation of a spirit tied to an infirm body. The novel's protagonist, who bears Welch's Christian name, Maurice, recalls Dante, who wrote of one who "awoke to find myself in a dark wood. . . . So bitter was it that death could be no worse,"[1] a soul who had to go through hell to reach purgatory and paradise. But Welch never lived to complete his novel, and the outcome of his character's torment is uncertain. During the course of his struggle, however, the protagonist did find human love, if not divine.

Maurice also recalls the figure of Job, whom God permitted the world, in the form of the Devil, to plague with boils in his very flesh. Like the Book of Job, Welch's *A Voice Through a Cloud* demonstrates the experience of pain as teacher, as revealer of ultimate truth. The experience is expecially difficult for Maurice, the artist, a sensitive person for whom the pain is most intense. When he looks into the mirror at his torn flesh, he sees the death of beauty, which for the artist is a spiritual death as well.

A Voice Through a Cloud is in many ways unique, like the *Divine Comedy* and the Book of Job, which it resembles in subject and vision. Through the ages sickness has been an unlikely subject for art, especially for the novel, which partially explains the sensation at the time of its publication of Tolstoy's *The Death of Ivan Illych* and also of Dostoevski's *The Idiot*. In our own time we remember Samuel

Beckett's trilogy in English, Thomas Mann's *The Magic Mountain,* perhaps Sylvia Plath's *The Bell Jar,* and only a few others. Since the rise of the novel, most novelists have concentrated on social rather than personal ills; and they have until recently, as in James Joyce, ignored the bodily functions as too crude or as too quotidian to warrant attention. In *A Voice Through a Cloud,* as John Updike has observed, "agony precedes psychology; introspection takes place only as pain's monopoly loosens. . . ."[2] Welch's last novel is basically an account of a man's crucifixion, ultimate suffering, pain, and death to the "ordinary" world of pretense, hypocrisy, and insincerity. Welch's "Maurice" is akin to Tolstoy's Ivan Illych in that both, in the primal experiences of pain and impending death, lose their "web of Maya," to borrow a phrase from Schopenhauer (who in turn borrowed it from Oriental philosophy). The phrase refers to the "solipsistic web which makes each individual secretly believe in his immortality and which prevents him from merging with his fellow humans in a mental flow of utter communion."[3]

Prior to an accident Maurice, like Ivan Illych, had spun around himself a web of deceit. A creature of vanity, he had deadened himself to humane values and had fooled himself into thinking he possessed a strong individuality. When he becomes one of many patients, all wearing identical gowns and suffering in identical beds, nature (or God) has its revenge. For, when Maurice needs help, sympathy, and understanding, he gets none—as when he wishes his classmate Mark would come see him. When Mark's absence causes Maurice to recall all the times he had abused Mark, Maurice finally realizes that he is subject to the same abuse and lies. At the novel's conclusion, as he ventures forth into the world, half cured and half ill, his broken Self has become an indistinguishable part of the universe. Instead of being splendidly independent, he must lean on his friends for what comfort there is. A new Maurice has been born through agony, and the course of events has caused him to lose his web.

In his search for identity, the novel's protagonist wears many guises. His dress changes from student clothes to a

hospital gown to his own pajamas to an alderman's robe
and finally to "normal" clothes. The shifts in his psyche
are also accompanied by changes in his name: at different
times he is known as Maurice, Sonny Boy, a bed number,
Ted, and finally Pusky.

His search for healing culminates in his meeting his ego
ideal, Dr. Farley, who is a Christ figure, a healer of the soul
as well as the body. The doctor is also an Apollo-Dionysus
figure: Apollo, in his capacity as doctor, practicing a conscious, objective skill in medicine; Dionysus, in his spontaneous, charismatic, "human" actions (as when he throws
the pineapple at Maurice). Maurice shares one perfect moment of communion with Dr. Farley during a walk on the
beach—one suspended moment of idealized doctor-patient
rapport—which later leads to disappointment and doubt.
Dr. Farley ultimately is guilty of being human, not divine,
as when he registers awkwardness and discomfort at entertaining the boy at tea in his new home. For Maurice, this
realization is a beneficial one; the patient is suddenly free
of dependence on the doctor, and he realizes for the first
time he must plan for living on his own.

II *The Artist as Job*

The development of this novel, Denton Welch's *mag-
num opus*, bears careful scrutiny. Each chapter is as fully
achieved as anything else Welch wrote, tight as "The Fire
in the Wood," beginning with the remarkable initial chapter. The accident itself is carefully foreshadowed several
times: In the inn where Maurice stops for tea, he suffers
"a vague, uneasy feeling of universal damage and loss"
(11);[4] and as he pedals his bicycle down the highway he
"felt pleased when I saw how well I managed the lights and
the cars." When the accident occurs, a boy whose father
nicknamed him "Safety First" is, ironically, the innocent
victim of another's carelessness.

Welch, who has been considered as not a novelist at all
by some critics, employed considerable novelistic skill to
communicate the shock of the accident. By abruptly shifting
from a description of traveling (on the bottom of page 12)
to a re-creation of the immediate aftermath of the collision

(top of page 13), the reader experiences the accident with Maurice as it occurred—suddenly and without warning—as he is hit from behind without even seeing anyone else on the road. Welch shows rather than tells, and the result is reality to an almost unbearable degree.

In the accident's aftermath Maurice recalls, "There was a confusion in my mind between being brought to life—forceps, navel-cords, midwives—and being put to death—ropes, axes, and black masks" (13). The confusion is generated by the death of one Self and by the birth of another. His web of Maya is totally rent, as this revealing passage indicates:

I tried to lull myself to sleep . . . but all the pleasant things that only yesterday I liked so much rose up to haunt me. I thought of eating delicious food, wearing good clothes, feeling proud and gay, going for walks, singing and dancing alone, fencing and swimming and painting pictures with other people, reading books. And everything seemed horrible and thin and nasty as soiled paper. I wondered how I could ever have believed in these things, how I could even for a moment have thought they were real. Now I knew nothing was real but pain, heat, blood, tingling, loneliness, and sweat. I began almost to gloat on the horror of my situation and surroundings. I felt paid out, dragged down, punished finally. Never again would my own good fortune make me feel guilty. I could look any beggars, blind people in the face now. Everything I had loved was disgusting; and I was disgusting too. (24-25)

While the voice through a cloud of the title is, literally, that of a policeman at the scene of the accident, it is also, as critic Ruby Cohn suggests, "The voice of the outer world, forming unclear words, empty of meaning if rich in sound; through the cloud of his anguish, Denton Welch has attempted to answer its questions and register its sound."[5]

The first hospital to which Maurice is taken bears the name of an ancient barbaric saint, and the barbarism is appropriate. His experience there is Kafka-like: the nurses and orderlies all seem hard, hard and heartless, incapable of sympathy (which means "feeling with"), let alone empathy, with the sick. And the spiritual malaise extends beyond the hospital to the representatives of the outside world who visit the patients. Relatives come bearing expressions of exasperation or boredom, and they are unaware that their own time for dependency is near. Welch's character of the dying journalist's wife is especially vivid, for she is more concerned about her loss of sleep than about her husband's health. It is significant that, when the girlfriend visits Dick, Maurice's wardmate, she symbolically has no ear; she is indifferent to his excessive speech which he uses as a defense against the hospital's inhumanity. To Maurice, the indifference of others is almost as unbearable as his physical pain: "Nothing was real but torture. Nobody seemed to realize that this was the only thing on earth. People didn't know that it was waiting for them quietly, patiently (18).

Instead of feeling like a patient, Maurice begins to feel more like a prisoner. The cruel x-ray nurse seems like an executioner; and because of the sadistic, evil natures of the hospital attendants, Maurice begins always to expect evil: "I had imagined human hearts as dried and shrivelled frogs before: now I thought of them as daffodil bulbs treacherously plump, full of black rottenness" (79). When the gray-haired old patient of his acquaintance attempts to escape from the hospital—only to find himself enclosed within a caged yard—the act is symbolic; for Welch is saying that we move from one form of entrapment to another. And the ball of wool that Maurice winds and unwinds in his bed is also symbolic: it represents his journey toward recovery, a journey which goes on and on and must be repeated just when the end is in sight.

At first, Maurice takes comfort in other's misfortunes, and enjoys squalor for its own sake. Any thoughts of beauty, he feels, would make a return to the reality of the world unbearable. As he loses more and more of his essential identity— wearing a uniform gown, eating uniform food, being renamed Ted—he finally seeks release in memories of the past. When squalor becomes reality, he seeks refuge in that other reality from which he has been separated by time. So complete is his dislocation that, when they move him from one hospital to another, leaving him temporarily out-of-doors in the world of the healthy, he confesses, "I don't know what anything is about" (54).

In the new hospital, his bed is located between the chimney and the lavatory. With one aperture leading heavenward, the other earthward, the setting is symbolic of his intermediary state: he now is about neither to die nor to be made well. The fellow patient Ray, with his half-paralyzed face, suggests a doppelganger for Maurice. And Ray's loss of knowledge of even the alphabet—basic human communication—signifies their total disorientation. His persistent question, "What is B?" might well be, "What is Being? What is life?"

At the new hospital, Maurice is inspired by a nurse. A figure of the artist, she makes beautiful lace while sitting through the night shift, creating beauty in the midst of horror. Maurice, weaving mental fantasies, now begins to resort to beauty for escape from hopelessness. Thoughts of romance and beauty replace his excursions into the past as the means of release from pain. He erases his present world by creating a new one: "Everything was made in my own image, and I was a sort of small God, keeping carefully within His own territory" (64). In the real world, he has turned briefly to Christian Science but it has held no answers for him. Even the hospital chaplain could offer no solace: "There was a desperation in his voice. He seemed to be complaining about the whole order of things—to be murmuring against God" (111).

But, rather than giving up, Maurice fights. Just as he combats horror with beauty, so does he insist upon altering his present lot. The turning point in his health (and in the novel) comes when he writes his brother to extricate him from the hospital and to place him in a private nursing home. Shortly after that symbolic step, he takes his first physical steps on his own; for, arrived in the nursing home and placed in a private room, he begins to become a Self again. And, when Dr. Farley, the village cynosure, proves to be sympathetic, Maurice really improves. When they walk on the beach together, amid the broken shells, Dr. Farley is like the Great Physician by the Sea of Galilee; and the shells are reminders of all the broken bodies and spirits of man he can heal. Indeed, the convalescent home matron and Maurice's aunt both possess what is described

as a "religious" attitude toward Dr. Farley. The relationship with the doctor helps Maurice perceptibly; he observes
in a metaphor of rebirth: "Surely I have been asleep . . .
blotted out by greyness and unreal horror, and now I'm
awakening. Hyacinth bulbs, when spring comes, suddenly
find that they are no longer degraded, crackling onions,
but stiff green towers, jangling with crisp bells and caught
in a trance of scent, heavy and swimming as chloroform"
(128). Maurice could be the new Lazarus; for, when he throws
away the rubber ferrule to his cane, his active act signals his
rebellion against sickness and death.

An important part of Maurice's renascence is the rebirth
of his art. Just as his body is rejuvenated by Dr. Farley, so
too are his creative powers. Fantasy is finally replaced
by actual creation when he finds he can paint again. One
of his first subjects is a urine specimen in a beaker, and the
inclusion of this detail in the novel is telling. First, the fact
that Maurice finds beauty in the visceral is a key to the Maur-
ice-Welch imagination. Secondly, in the act of creating art,
Maurice is building a new life from his shattered past; and
Welch was intuitively, if not intellectually, correct about
his choice of symbol: a urine specimen is the ancient alchemical symbol of healing.[6] And, third, the painting acts as a
catalyst: Dr. Farley's reaction of disgust to the artist's subject dramatizes the basic difference between their two tem-
peraments. However, as an artist, Maurice is always mis-
understood. When he briefly appears in public in the scarlet
alderman's robe he uses as dressing gown—an outward and
visible sign of his artistic and spiritual nature—he is stoned
by a villager.

Dr. Farley also disappoints Maurice. The youth has a
premonition of the doctor's imperfection (his humanity)
through the role the physician plays in in the amateur the-
atrical. Appearing to be counterfeit and moving about a
world with trembling walls, the doctor is contemplated
from afar—framed in the proscenium—and found to be
totally unheroic. Viewed in this rational perspective, Dr.
Farley is seen to be as imperfect as anyone else. (Physician,
heal thyself.) This realization, which upsets Maurice,
causes him to have a relapse. When he later confesses his

uneasiness about the permanence of his relationship to the doctor, the confession is a mistake; it ruptures their relations in a way that causes Dr. Farley to be more distant forever after. Maurice cannot accept things as they are; he wants only to believe in some idealized version of reality.

Dr. Farley's attempt at finding Maurice a friend more his own age also is a failure. Maurice rejects cozy conventionality in favor of brief encounters with outcasts and wanderers with whom he feels an affinity. After his relationship with the doctor, he wants to observe mankind coldly from the outside, rather than to become involved; but coming too close invariably involves disappointment. He projects his thoughts into the mid-Victorian painting in his aunt's house: the family group depicted there had been thoroughly romanticized by the artist, he decides. His experience tells him that "There was probably in reality a costive heaviness in the air; those children would have been quarrelling; that collie would have smelled; the bride's father would have been thinking of his kidney disease, or his money; the bride herself would have suffered from the tightness of her stays and the fear of the spot that was threatening to appear on her chin" (197).

Finally, Dr. Farley actually lets Maurice down. After having alluded to letting the youth come live with him and his wife in their new home, he never mentions the offer again; indeed, he even seems discommoded by the prospect of even having him live in the same village. Maurice would like to be a solipsist still, but he is forced by his health to depend on others. When Dr. Farley fails him, he leans upon a Miss Keziah Hellier. As discussed in Chapter I of this study, Miss Hellier is based upon a real acquaintance of Welch's; and he doubtless chose the fictitious name "Keziah" not so much to protect his friend (Miss Evie Sinclair) as to embody her character with all the biblical connotations of the name, since Keziah was one of the daughters of Job who gave the afflicted man comfort in his later years. (It is not inconceivable that Denton Welch felt that he too was Job.) In the novel, Miss Hellier's eyes "bore a curious surface likeness to Dr. Farley's" (239); therefore, in his search for a relationship of stability and significance, Maurice chose in Miss Hellier a surrogate for the saintly doctor. On the last page, the pair is searching for a suitable place to begin a new life together; and the focus shifts from the struggle for life to the struggle for shelter.

III *Conclusion*

Thus the novel ends, incomplete. Yet, despite the fact that it is unfinished, the book seems remarkably whole since there is little more that Welch could have added to portray the plight of the protagonist. It is not a perfect work of art— few novels ever are; but, toward the end, A *Voice Through a Cloud* seems to ramble, as if Welch, fighting against time and fever in his fatal sickness, did not quite know how to terminate the book. And the last quarter becomes more obviously novelistic than all that preceded; for characters formerly introduced, such as Mark, somewhat gratuitously reappear.

But whatever its faults, A *Voice Through a Cloud* is Denton Welch's most mature work. In its writing he found a spiritual rapport with his characters which was lacking in *Maiden Voyage* and *In Youth Is Pleasure*, books in which the protagonist, Welch, had been too much the dilettante— the precocious observer of life rather than the involved participant. Certainly the novel repudiates the charge leveled by both G. S. Fraser and Edmund Wilson that Welch's work was flawed by an evasion of real problems and that it treated specialized aspects of life rather than life as a whole.[7] In this book, life itself is now Welch's subject—life and the struggle to preserve it against awesome odds.

Shortly after its publication, Francis Wyndham said A *Voice Through a Cloud* was "as likely to survive as anything published since the war."[8] In 1966, John Updike was able to proclaim it "a prophetic document" and to conclude: "in an age quick to label any sufficiently bleak and sententious novel 'existential,' here is a work by an author born again out of agony into the world, that seems to reconstitute the raw elements of existence."[9] The book *is* existential, and it bears comparison with the mature novels of both Sartre and Camus, as my Chapter 9 indicates. From his sickness, Denton Welch created "a work of art spun like a delicately lovely spider's web out of his own entrails."[10]

CHAPTER 6

The Later Stories: **A Last Sheaf**

MANY of Welch's characteristic topics and themes recur in *A Last Sheaf*, the second and posthumous collection of his shorter pieces. Among the book's concerns are the themes of isolation and alienation, the tension between the heterosexual and the homosexual principles, the relationship of characters to the past, the role of the artist in society, the disparity between appearance and reality, and the changing face of England as she approached the middle of the twentieth century. The effects of World War II are felt in this book more than in any other Welch wrote save the *Journals*. And, for the first time, there is an explicit expression of his belief in the supernatural. New sexual freedom and narrow human selfishness also pervade the book. To a much greater degree than in *Brave and Cruel*, the tone is one of pessimism: a recurring image in *A Last Sheaf* is that of humans as bottles full of bile, waiting to be uncorked.

The book is, to be sure, a mixed bag. It contains not only the nine uncollected short stories, but also the journalistic account of Welch's visit to the painter Walter Sickert (1860-1942)—that selfsame account which had caught Dame Edith's condorlike eye when it originally appeared in *Horizon*; a seventy-six page fragment of a novel; sixty-seven poems; and reproductions of nine of his paintings besides various book decorations.

The novel fragment, on which Welch spent nearly two years' work before abandoning it, is considered in the next chapter (together with his other known incomplete novel, *I Left My Grandfather's House*). And the poems, for which Welch had so earnestly wished separate book publication, are considered in a chapter with his other important incidental writing, *The Journals*. But the journalistic piece on Sickert might well be considered along with his stories since

Welch usually walked that fine line between fact and fancy, reportage and fiction, and since the method he employed in recording his "interview" with Sickert scarcely varies from the method behind the "stories."

The Sickert piece is reportage raised to the level of art, as Dame Edith perceived when she wrote to the young author after reading it: "I cannot tell you how much my brother Osbert, with whom I am staying, and I, enjoyed your alarming experience with Mr. Sickert. We laughed till we cried—though really in some ways it was no laughing matter. But one thing came out very clearly, and that is, that you are a *born writer.* . . . Nothing could have been more admirable, for instance, than your description of the stringy man who was about to lose his hair. . . ."[1] Dame Edith was quite right in that the Sickert piece is more serious than frivolous; for, as in all of Welch's writings, the author has seen the skull beneath the flesh.

I   *"Sickert at St. Peter's"*

"Sickert at St. Peter's" is an artful piece in which Welch strikingly contrasts gentility and crudity. Both extremes were present in Walter Sickert, according to Welch's account; and Welch dramatizes both. Rather than entering the great man's house through a foyer, according to Welch, one entered through a watercloset—a detail that most likely was factual. But taking the floor plan as emblematic of the man, Welch describes Sickert's boots as "great sewer-boots."[2] The scatology continues, as, when Mrs. Sickert's guest departs, Sickert is talking of some condition in which he "couldn't pass water for six days!" (13).

Sickert prides himself upon his sensitivity as an artist and proclaims of his work, "That picture gives you the right feeling, doesn't it? You'd kiss your wife like that if you'd just come up from the pit, wouldn't you?" But he is revealed ultimately to be quite insensitive as a human being. His disregard for others is summarized poetically by Welch: when the boys are ready for departure, "Sickert dragged on our coats as if he were dressing sacks of turnips" (17).

With admirable precision Welch reveals in a very few pages many facets of a complex man, a man who is exposed as boorish, hypochondriac, sentimental, and quite possibly paranoid. After publication of the work, there were numerous uneasy souls in England, all hoping that Mr. Denton Welch would not come to "interview" them. But there was no cause for alarm. Welch's obsession with his own personality and past was so consuming that the Sickert visit was the only journalistic piece he was to publish.

II *"The Earth's Crust"*

"The Earth's Crust" is the monologue of a lonely art student, and as such is related to the novel fragment of art-student days also included in the volume. The protagonist of "The Earth's Crust" is a romantic, and the story telescopes within one typical day the events leading to his confrontation with the reality he has always avoided. The student, a chronic reader, uses literature as a method of escape. One book he reads is Butler's *The Way of All Flesh*—a title that is singularly appropriate since the rooming house in which he reads it is a microcosm of the macrocosm. He observes with compassion the furtive, futile existences of the adults in this city rooming house, and he contrasts their lives with the wild abandon of the suburban children he encounters on his way to art school. He is reluctant to admit that life must be so bleak once responsibilities are assumed.

Yet there seems to him no other conclusion. His bus passes sweat shops, factories, even an asylum—various manifestations of "the way of all flesh." He formulates a world view which is quite bitter: "Along the pavements thronged the people, like bottles walking; their heads as inexpressive as round stoppers. What if some god or giant should bend down and take several of the stoppers out? I thought. Inside there would be black churning depths like bile, or bitter medicine" (19-20). The story is filled with such images of revulsion and despair, dominated by the color black: the black bile in people, the black eels slowly dying on zinc trays in the shop window—the lives of eels and people being equally paltry and fruitless.

When the protagonist, in a moment of depression, seeks succor from a friend, he finds the friend's door locked, the place empty. The scene is a statement on the isolation of man: one is always and inevitably alone; there is no one to help make life any easier or less bleak. Finally, the protagonist, the prototypical man, sees lovers lying in the park; but they appear flimsy, "like trash washed up on a beach, or corpses in an old war photograph" (23). Man and trash are one, as the atrocities of war have demonstrated by making life so cheap.

To the protagonist, love clearly does not provide a solution to man's loneliness. In support of his feelings, is a lover's quarrel, one that demonstrates the way of the world, that he witnesses. Just the night before, the couple had been lovers; "Now they were murderous, searching for the worst poison and the sharpest pain" (25). And, when the woman sticks out her tongue at her lover, it "flashed out like a serpent's" (25)—an image that related to the serpentine eels earlier in the story. Witnessing this cruel quarrel, the art student has an epiphany: this is the way of the world, full of hate and spite and misery. No amount of reading romantic novels or painting pretty pictures can change for him now the world as he has seen it: "In my dismay it seemed to me as if the earth's crust had cracked and I had looked through and seen reality at last" (25). This moment of epiphany is rare in Welch's stories, which usually build their point cumulatively rather than climatically.

III   *"Memories of a Vanished Period"*

"Memories of a Vanished Period" is a tale populated by sexual deviates and madmen, and their extreme conditions are symbolic of the abnormal tenor of the times during World War II. The story also compares the innocence and freshness of youth with the degeneracy and horrors of old age, as does the preceding story. That age has a claim, a hold upon youth, is symbolically conveyed in the scene when the mother pinches the bride on her wedding day.

The memoir tells what it was like to be young and drunk and to have all of London drunk with one during wartime. It graphically portrays the hedonism and madness that occur on the homefront when there is war waging on the battlefield. During the fragile tale, the youthful protagonist visits an underground bar where he encounters numerous homosexuals and degenerates. Welch expresses here not so much aversion to sexual abnormality as contempt for all those with pretensions and self-delusions, whatever form they may take.

Trapped in London during an air raid, the youth goes to the house of a friend, where he meets Michael, a madman who seeks refuge from reality by constant reexamination of his past. Michael is a caricature of all Englishmen on the homefront during that period in history. Values have lost all meaning; the present is confusing; the future, unthinkable; and the only solace is the past. The narrator summarizes the period with the phrase, "Loonies within and Nazis without."

Unlike "The Earth's Crust," however, this story does not conclude with the protagonist in despair. After the air raid ceases, paper fragments fall like snow. The factual explanation is that some paper mills had been bombed, but the poetical truth is that the sight of the burnt falling ashes is like the benediction of an Ash Wednesday, an outward and visible sign of peace slowly falling. Suddenly everything "seemed new, saved, relished again" (38). After the war, things will be better; after the war, normality will return to the land.

IV "A Fragment of a Life Story"

Such easy optimism is not present in the succeeding tale, "A Fragment of a Life Story," in which Welch uses the symbolic act of viewing an old and battered religious film which has become dim and hard to see as the means to convey man's loss of belief and values in our time. The narrator cannot bear to watch the film; he already is possessed by a terrible sense of *déjà vu*. His personal philosophy envisions the world governed by some demiurge: "I looked up at the spire of St. Stephen's Church. It appeared to me as a huge sharpened stake, put there by God for an instrument of torture. I imagined a gigantic body hurtling down from heaven and landing on this spike, pierced through the belly, the arms and legs spread-eagled and turning like windmills in their agony . . ." (40).

The narrator's friend, on the other hand, glories in the

film. Touchette actually mocks the crucifixion scene and its message, reveling in the melodramatic "thunder and lightning effects;" (45). Touchette's blasphemy, coupled with the narrator's own betrayal by his doctor friend, ignites a will to self-destruction in him. The doctor's betrayal (a situation reminiscent of that in *A Voice Through a Cloud*), when viewed in conjunction with the film of the Lord's Passion, suggests that the narrator sees himself as a contemporary Christ figure who is denied and betrayed, one who now must inevitably meet his own death. (See the remarks on Christian allegory in *Maiden Voyage* which conclude Chapter 2 of this study for some interesting parallels.)

The world in which the martyred protagonist finds himself is a very sick one, and sickness is conveyed by the imagery Welch has used to support his theme. The nicotine stains on Touchette's fingers, teeth, and nose—the yellow color of decay—are the taint of the world which envelop everything, and his name connoting "touch," suggests that everything he comes in contact with likewise will be spoiled. As a result, he attempts suicide but his attempt ends only in embarrassment and failure. There are no easy outs; and, like everything else in the story, his act is but a mere parody of what it should be. To paraphrase Eliot, we are all hollow men, stuffed with straw; and the narrator is left to face this terrible world on its own terms.

V   "A Party"

The Proceedings of the Sexual Reform Congress is one of the books the lonely art student, Ian, sees in the home where he attends a bohemian masquerade in "A Party." Ostensibly Welch cites this volume, along with others, to indicate the catholic taste of the book collector, Baby. But the book's title serves as a key to the story's theme as well: sexual liberation and license. This theme is also supported by the recurring descriptions of the hostess' cats at their sexual play. Welch establishes an ironic counterpoint, for the party guests inside behave with no more inhibitions than the cats outside.

Rather Prufrockian by inclination, Ian attends the party masqueraded ironically as Bacchus, whose spirit is invoked throughout the story. Ian is, however, by inclination the least bacchanalian of individuals; and his insecurity is manifested in his dread of losing all his hair, a fear we can interpret as his fear of emasculation: the shorn Samson was one sapped of all his manly strength. During the party, games are played, and at one point the lights are extinguished. In the dark, Ian has physical contact with one of the guests who is disguised as a nun. The "nun," however, proves to be a young man whose female attire is a clue to his sexual inversion. Missing his last bus home, Ian accepts the "nun's" invitation to spend the night. The time is passed innocently enough, and Ian thinks he may finally have found a companion. Yet the other youth's earlier gropings in the dark were as instinctive and impermanent as when the cat scratched Ian. The youth and the cats are all creatures of instinct, scratching a prurient itch; and Ian will be hurt ultimately and once more left alone.

VI *"Evergreen Seaton-Leverett"*

"Evergreen Seaton-Leverett" is a character study of an English eccentric and a pungent statement about the transitory nature of human relations. It is very well written in its exquisite detail and its careful counterpoint between appearance and reality. When the reader first glimpses Evergreen, she seems a public figure enjoying an outing; but when the narrator visits her at home, we realize how inwardly directed Evergreen really is.[3] She lives solely in the past and for the past. She has, for example, saved all her old party invitations from decades ago, when she was young and popular: "Invitations to garden parties, dinners, weddings, balls and christenings. All were yellowed, curling at the corners and thick with furry dust, so that they had an almost artificial air . . ." (72). Evergreen rather reminds one of Dickens's Miss Havisham; both are prisoners of the past.

The narrator deeply resents the attitude of the villagers who find their amusement in ridiculing Evergreen. The narrator sees her not as a figure of fun but as one to be pitied, perhaps, and certainly as one worth getting to know. He even thinks her lies are excusable and probably necessary: we all need our illusions in order to make life liveable. Evergreen prevaricates and hides from the world, yet there is something eternal about her: like the tree from which her nickname is derived, she has continued to prosper through all seasons. As if sensing this relation, she dresses her chauffeur and footman in symbolic dark green as well.

But the narrator's desire to get to know Evergreen is not fulfilled. She dies and takes with her the romantic secret of her life. No matter what our various ruses to manage to live life, we cannot escape mortality.

VII "A Picture in the Snow"

Danny, in "A Picture in the Snow," is an unfulfilled artist figure. When he walks around the overgrown grounds of his former home, he is the Minotaur exploring the labyrinth of self. The huge empty house is a symbol of Danny's empty life, with all the early promise evacuated. Instead of the artist he could have been, he is now a lazy, lost dilettante. His creativity has lost all spark, and he is like the "forlorn lamppost" near his home with which he can be identified, an object "with broken glass and empty bulb socket; leaves surged up to smother it" (85).

But Danny has in many ways been the victim of circumstances. With an absentee father and an alcoholic mother, he seems at times in a state of arrested childhood. On one level, his visitation to the old house is an active search to recapture the lost past. On another level, the story is an allegory for the changing face of England, an England in which no one can now afford to support a great home except the state itself. When Danny's house finally falls into disrepair, only to be saved by becoming an institution, graceless and sterile, with modern cubelike buildings built in the once beautiful garden, we have a formidable allegory about the passing of the old order and the establishment of the new.

VIII "Ghosts"

Transparent in intention and execution, "Ghosts" is a simple piece that does not demand explication.[4] It suffices to say the tale is a fictionalized account of the writing of Welch's first story—a ghost story for a school assignment. "Ghosts" reveals how the exotic and the roccoco absorbed his imagination at even an early age. It also contains one of the few explicit references to the supernatural in his writings outside *A Voice Through a Cloud* (cf. Chapter 18 of that novel), though Eric Oliver has told us of Welch's strong belief in the existence of Ghosts.[5]

IX *"The Hateful Word"*

In editing *A Last Sheaf*, Eric Oliver and John Lehmann were very astute in leaving the best for last. "The Hateful Word"—the penultimate story—and "The Diamond Badge" —which concludes the selection, represent Denton Welch in top form. Both employ the Albertine strategy of "The Fire in the Wood," and "The Hateful Word" even approaches the artistry of that story. Like "The Fire in the Wood," it is a very Laurentian tale in plot and manner, recalling the force and sexual drive behind, say, Lawrence's "The Prussian Officer," and the insidious triangle explored several times by Lawrence, as in his "The Old Adam."

Welch's protagonist, Flora Pinkston, is a restless woman of middle age. The name is key to the woman: she is like a flower, a vital life force, in the pink of health and the prime of life. Furthermore, the color pink is instructive concerning her nature, which is sensual. Her mental state is mirrored in that of her garden in which she takes much pride: at the beginning of the story, "the garden looked a little bedraggled. The grass was rather too long and a few weeds had sprung up in the borders" (101). But, after the young soldier Harry enters her life, the garden is made tidy and beautiful again.[6]

When Flora first sees Harry, she projects her own loneliness upon him. Actually, it is she who craves company and not Harry. Just as he is a prisoner of war, Flora is a prisoner of marriage, which has lost all meaning for her. Flora's feelings for Harry, on the other hand, are strong and complex. Her reason for asking him home, in an act which constitutes a common pickup, is at least subconsiously, if not consciously, an act of sexual aggression. The very act of paying him for working in her garden gives her a kind of sexual pleasure. In a very real way, the garden is Flora herself, which Harry tills. But there is also something very maternalistic in Flora's attitude's. She admires his "compact doll-like quality"; and she contrasts his smallness favorably with her husbands's bulk. She even keeps her liquor in a doll's house—and adult pleasure is concealed behind a childish facade, another manifestation of her (and Welch's) fascination with the diminutive.

However maternalistic the childless Flora's feelings, it is the role of lover and not son which she wishes Harry to assume. For Harry to love her would be confirmation of her beauty and the continuation of her powers to appeal; for Flora lives in horror of losing her charm to middle age, of her face's coming to look like (a marvelous image, borrowed from Joyce Cary) "a chamber daubed with strawberry jam" (104).[7] When her advance to Harry is repelled, Flora is deeply hurt; her entire image of self is at stake. And, when Harry tells her, "You are like mother to me—my English mother," she is crushed. *Mother* is the hateful word which, once uttered, prevents her from ever having romantic illusions about herself again.

X *"The Diamond Badge"*

In "The Diamond Badge," a parable on human selfishness, Susan Innes, the narrator, is a young woman who writes the author of a book she has just read to ask if she may meet him. A date is arranged; and, when she visits the author—Andrew Clifton, she is surprised to find him a dwarf and attended by a young man her own age whom Andrew obviously loves. We might be tempted to inflict a biographical interpretation on the story, as Maurice Cranston suggests, because Andrew's deformity could be an interpolation of Welch's: "He was terribly deformed, his hands all twisted and his body seemingly telescoped into itself, so that he was broad, but perhaps only three feet tall. He had a smooth oval face with rather delicate features. His hair was red and a little silky fringe ran right round his jaw line, framing his face and making him look a particularly well-groomed ill-disposed monkey."

As Cranston agrees, this portrait is a monstrously distorted one of Welch, if self-portraiture were intended. The description might well communicate, however, how Welch feared others saw him in his incapacity. "And as such," Cranston concludes, "it underlines his most conspicuous failing: he had no trust. This connects in turn with his greatest limitation as an artist. He built too many barricades and enclosed the range of his understanding."[8] Indeed, the absence of trust is the very theme of "A Diamond Badge."

During the protagonist's overnight stay, the beginnings of a triangle are formulated. Susan experiences affection for Tom Parkinson, Andrew's companion; and, when Tom comes to her room at night with the pretext that she has called out in her sleep, she suspects he feels somewhat the same. When Tom adjusts her blanket, his arms linger about her. When Andrew intrudes, Tom even leaves his arms there longer than necessary, as if to proclaim his affection and to admit he is not ashamed of it.

Not wishing to intrude further upon Tom and Andrew in her confused state of mind, Susan decides early the next morning to slip away before the household awakens. But, to ensure a return visit, or at least to promote further correspondence, she decides to leave "accidentally" her little diamond pin in the guest room where it will be found. But neither man writes to her about finding it, and not until much later in the year is this silence explained. When she happens upon a new story by Andrew in a magazine, it is based upon her visit and the transparency of her plot with the pin. When Andrew finally returns the diamond badge, the pin and the act seem of no value to Susan any longer. The loss of trust and value is emphasized by the telling detail of Andrew's failure to insure or register the parcel, another violation of values.

Susan perceives from the published story that Andrew's actions, which at the time had seemed harmless and childlike, were in actuality deliberate. He had "used" her while she visited and afterward as a means to break his writer's block and to secure material for his fiction. Ironically, Susan had been just as calculating but in a different way. She had used her visit to satisfy her curiosity, intruding upon Andrew's private life out of a whim. And even Tom's action of leaving his hands upon her in the presence of Andrew can, in retrospect, be interpreted as a mean and selfish act if Tom deliberately attempted to invoke the dwarf's jealousy.

Andrew's physical deformity is symbolic of his psychological state: his psyche is stunted and underdeveloped; he has failed to grow as a human and as an artist. As an artist figure, his deformity also is appropriate: the fact he has written a book makes him a nonconformist or misfit of sorts, and the very act of its publication subjects him to public view, not unlike a figure in a sideshow. The diamond badge, on the other hand, is a symbol of all values and gifts which are betrayed. The diamond traditionally is the gem signifying love; in this case, it is emblematic of betrayal.

The triangle which might have been between two lovers and one beloved becomes, instead, a triangle of triple treachery. The ultimate irony remains that Susan has been just as selfish as Andrew and Tom. She visited for selfish reasons, disliked Andrew for selfish reasons (thinking him a "little dumpy figure," his robe like "a fat tube of toothpaste with the used part neatly rolled up"), and she used Tom. Andrew's retaliation was merely retribution.

"The Diamond Badge" is, therefore, a comment about the way we use people to our own advantage, taking from them what we will with little or no regard for their feelings. It is a fitting finale to that group of stories which constitutes Denton Welch's last because, in its way, it is the most mature story of the several about artists and writers in *A Last Sheaf*. Just as the majority of stories in *Brave and Cruel* concerned childhood or very early adolescence, so the second collection contains a majority about young artists. Welch had focused his inward vision to a later period in life. While the second collection may not be so consistently well-achieved technically as the first, it nevertheless rewards the reader.

CHAPTER 7

The Unfinished Novels:
I Left My Grandfather's House
and A Novel Fragment

I Song of Innocence

THE dichotomy between Welch's early and late work is well illustrated by the two novels-in-progress that he left at the time of his death. *I Left My Grandfather's House* was written as a rough draft, abandoned by the author in the spring of 1943, and not published until 1958 when the manuscript was discovered among his papers and was printed in its original form.[1] *A Novel Fragment*, on the other hand, while begun in January, 1944, continued to absorb Welch at least until the summer of 1945 and quite possibly longer. Unlike *Grandfather's House*, it shows evidence of conscious craftmanship and a concern for novelistic technique. In a letter to T. Murray Ragg, then managing editor of Routledge, Welch called it, "The best I have done so far!"[2]

To name a 1943 work "Early Welch" and a 1945 work "Late" may seem foolhardy in view of such creative spans as Somerset Maugham's, who produced *Liza of Lambeth* in 1897 and *The Razor's Edge* in 1944. But we must remember that Welch's entire writing career totaled but seven years. Being bedridden, however, he was able to produce more during any month than some writers achieve in a year. And the books written between the beginning of 1943 and the conclusion of 1945 are evidence enough that Denton Welch's artistic vision underwent a change.

In the earlier fiction, works like *Maiden Voyage*, "The Barn," and *Grandfather's House*, the protagonist's quest for experience is conducted with singular innocence—an innocence almost total in its frankness and lack of inhibition. These works are written with what Walter Allen has called "an astonishingly pure response to the sensual surface of things."[3] Throughout Welch's writing career his language maintained its freshness, but the vision informing the language changed, as a comparison between *Maiden Voyage* and *In Youth Is Pleasure* reveals. The world of childhood and promise of the earlier books is displaced by the world of illness and infirm adulthood in *A Voice through a Cloud*. And in that book, as well as in the stories in *A Last Sheaf* and in *A Novel Fragment*, the once total innocence is displaced by sketchily concealed eroticism. This eroticism is especially perceived in *In Youth Is Pleasure* and in those works that concern Welch's years at art school—the story "A Party" and the novel fragment. When read together, "A Party" seems an exercise in preparation for the writing of that incomplete novel.

As does *In Youth is Pleasure*, both construe the experiential quest for self-discovery in sexual terms, as might be expected since the protagonist (named Ian in "A Party" and Robert in *A Novel Fragment)* is in late adolescence. As in the novels of Forrest Reid, adolescence and the act of attaining manhood in Welch's fiction rarely generate an expansion of the protagonist's sensibility; there is, instead, a sense of emotional constriction, something altogether the opposite of growth. Instead of the malleable and adventuresome Denton of *Maiden Voyage*, we are given the prim and inverted Robert of *A Novel Fragment*—and the difference is that between early and late Welch.

I Left My Grandfather's House is pure, early Welch. A straightforward and almost artless account of the author's first walking tour, this work is distinguished by uncluttered writing and by the total absence of symbols and sexual psychology. While appearing the least novelistic of his longer fictions, the episodic book does have a certain thematic unity and controlling vision. Like *Maiden Voyage*, the voyage of the protagonist is an experiential one. The boy Denton has what he interprets to be several brushes with death, one through contact with a desperate-looking hobo (5) and another when he encounters quicksand (38). During his picaresque journey, he also falls victim to a young farmer who tries to con him out of money (32); and he witnesses with fascination two swans making love (11). Death, chicanery, cruelty, and sex are four experiences which impress themselves most vividly on the young boy.

But, during his walking tour, he is something more than a mere receiver of whatever life transmits to him; he is actively evaluating the people he meets. In this respect, the book's protagonist resembles the narrator of Bunyan's *Pilgrim's Progress,* that soul who began his story with the words, "As I walk'd through the wilderness of this world, I lighted on a certain place where was a Den, and laid me down in that place to sleep. . . ."[4] The words and the tone roughly correspond with Welch's beginning, "As I walked, I thought, 'I've really started now, and I don't know where I am going to sleep tonight' " (1). Both Welch's and Bunyan's protagonists leave families to undertake individual journeys; both open themselves to experience; both judge those they encounter by individual reactions to themselves and to their respective quests—Bunyan's spiritual, and Welch's esthetic. Both narrators demonstrate great courage in the face of adversity. The young Denton especially is shown as a Job-figure, being ridiculed by the insensitive for his physical appearance; and this identification with Job was continued, as we have seen in *A Voice Through a Cloud.*

There are great differences, however, between Bunyan's book and Welch's incomplete novel. Bunyan's is a strict allegorical "progress," but Welch's Denton returns home for money and has "no plan, no looking-forward feeling. I was dead inside, with no adventurousness" (72). It is instructive nevertheless to compare the people both narrators meet—Bunyan's are types whose very names reveal their failings or their virtues (Neighbor Pliable, Mr. Fearing, etc.); Welch's are individuals who are also a mixed bag of good and bad who become types as they reveal themselves to him. As it happens, perhaps the best and kindest person Denton encounters is a Bishop who performs spontaneously the one pure, joyous action in the book—the throwing of the bread (30), an act of revelation which parallels Dr. Farley's throwing of the pineapple in *A Voice Through a Cloud*. Denton perceives the Bishop's beauty, which is not the least bit physical.

In a very real way, *I Left My Grandfather's House* also recalls Chaucer's *Canterbury Tales*. At one point, Denton considers taking the Pilgrim's Way to Canterbury, but the map is smudgy and the way difficult, and the youth loses himself en route. And the various characters Denton encounters remind us of Chaucer's Pilgrims as well as Bunyan's, those Chaucerian characters who were individuals within types, whereas Welch's characters are individuals who become types.

During the boy's quixotic travels he encounters many who are physically beautiful, but he sees that morally most are not. He experiences pain at seeing "some beautifully-made intricate thing threatened" (74), as when he notices the beautiful male swimmer's missing tooth and grieves that this image of God has been broken by dissipation. Denton's walking tour is, in its way, unconsciously religious; and the protagonist is disappointed in mankind: most people fail to show any hospitality or welcome to a stranger. However, the book ends on a hopeful note. The jolly man Denton meets last (80) is a good omen and a friendly gate-keeper to the future. The book ends but does not conclude, for the tour is to continue indefinitely, with hope and joy, despite past discouragements.

Besides the moral and theological concerns of the short novel, there are implicit treatments of the role of the artist in society. Denton correctly sees the artist as a monk-figure, but his version of the monastic life is a highly romanticized one: "I should have a stone cell in a garden with honey bees buzzing close to me in an old rush-woven hive, and with enormous sun flowers nodding their black faces along my hedge; . . . I should have a crystal crucifix and the loveliest old primitive that money could extort from its original monastery; . . . I should have a gushing spring and delicious food from heaven . . ." (45-46).

The youth, of course, has been unable to separate his love of material things from the attractions (for him) of leading the contemplative life. His version of what a monastery should be is related to his urges throughout the book to re-store whatever old ruin he sees, to make it into his own palacial dwelling. But the reader comes to understand that Denton's values, while somewhat confused, will define themselves for the better. The boy's last act in the book is to paint a church, and he takes his greatest pleasure in the artistic creation: "For once I felt almost delighted" (82), he confesses; and the reader delights with him.

II   *Song of Experience*

I Left My Grandfather's House, then, is a celebration of nat-ural and manmade beauty. *A Novel Fragment* is something else altogether, a lamentation on "the way of all flesh." Fleshly images are everywhere in the book, starting with the repellent image of the model, Madame David, with which Welch begins the novel:

The sight of all that mauvish flesh with the hank of dark hair sent a tingle of horror right through his body . . . . Those heavy tubes which were her arms and legs—how was he to relate them to that swelling stomach and torso? The breasts, curved and globular as the breakfast-cups on the L.M.S. Railways, seemed impossibly difficult, with their nightmarishly large purple-pink nipples. He felt dimly that there must be something wrong with the nipples, that they must be swollen; he was even afraid that before the end of the lesson they would have spread a little further up the smooth white globes of flesh.[5]

This strong revulsion is more than Welch's usual misog-ynistic reaction. The image of the fleshly model is related to that of butcher's meat which the protagonist Robert later sees on display, illuminated by unpleasant pink lights: "The warm boudoir-pink glow made the raw pieces of dead animal even more horrible" (140). The adjective "boudoir-pink" is interesting, for the dead meat is equated with a lady's bed-room. Appropriately enough, Robert is an art student—one who interprets the reality around him. For Robert, reality is the universal mauvish gray of the art room, a world covered with clay dust and a place where flaccid bodies are displayed like meat. A one point in the novel, Robert quite literally sees the world through "distorting, mauvish glass;" and Robert's distorted world view sees decay in every form. The color mauve pervades the novel everywhere—the color of decadence combines with frequent allusions to Beardsley and Wilde to complete the portrait of the life of decadent artists.

Robert, whose nickname "Sonny" indicates his infantilism rather than a bright and cheerful outlook, is a misogynist whose views are echoed by the "Reverand Parker," a character who delivers a polemic against his fiancée: "It's frightful, Miss Calthrop; a man feels tied hand and foot when his fiancée keeps collecting more and more stuff together. I'm quite weighed down under all her wardrobes and carpets and toast-racks" (145-46).

When another art student, Gerald Hope, intrudes into Robert's life,[6] his surname is a misnomer, for Gerald presents no hope for Robert. Gerald is easily more cynical: his painting of a human eye in a cage is symbolic of himself in his house at Queen's Grove as he critically surveys the world without and around him. Hope is more overtly homosexual and possibly also masochistic: as a child, his brother practiced sadistic games on him, which he still relates; and his room is festooned with ropes and boots and a riding crop. When Hope plays "The Merry, Merry Pipes of Pan" on the piano, it is an overture which upsets Robert immensely. Hope, a perverted Pan figure, is chasing the helpless maiden Robert, whose Victorian morals cause him to despise the tune more than any other he can think of.

As Robert and Hope journey through the novel together, they observe all manner of evil, and Welch's imagery is given full vent in describing the cruelties of nature—as when they see "Winter aconites with petals unpleasantly like the stiff wings torn off poor beetles" (158); or when a capon cat bites Robert; or when a wrestler tells him how other wrestlers try to gouge out his eyes. As if to arm themselves against such a predatory world, both Robert and Hope bear sticks on their travels: Robert's is a silver-knobbed cane and Hope's an umbrella. But the totem-phalluses do not work; both boys are helpless against brute masculine force, and at one point the wrestler symbolical-ly carries Robert off on his shoulder like a Sabine woman about to be raped.

Another phallic symbol brought to play in the novel is the priest's staff on Ash Wednesday. When the Protestant Robert is touched on the forehead by it, he experiences an excitement almost sexual in nature and intensity. The sexual and the theological become one at several points in the novel, as when Robert is reconciled with Hope over Easter weekend, the season of man's hope and belief in the resurrection of the dead. (We recall Welch also set the story "The Coffin on the Hill," on Easter weekend for similar symbolic and ironic purposes.)

Despite this auspicious reconciliation, Robert is unful-filled by the friendship, just as he is unfulfilled as an artist. He allows himself to be picked up on a bus by a stranger, John Russell, who later proves to possess a formidable anx-iety neurosis. One of his most unhappy experiences has been a short term in the military; and, when he gives a photograph of himself as a soldier to Robert, the act is an attempt at shucking his past. But Robert is not able to find happiness in the company of Russell any more than he is with Hope, and it is a symbolic gesture when Russell mis-treats Robert's stick.

Although incomplete, the novel works toward a climax both meet and right. At the art students' costume ball, we have an apocalyptic vision of Hell on earth. The human condition is depicted in the murals which decorate the dance hall: "The whole effect was of some grizzly fair ground, where half-dismembered bodies and screaming mouths met the gaze at every turn" (192). Welch has sustained the butcher-meat imagery in this description of the dance as being like "a cannibal butcher's shop" (193).

Robert's costume for the ball, composed of items both clerical and secular, represent the division which is within him. Furthermore, the costume's overall color, purple, is symbolic of his perversion and passion—the culmination of all the mauve tones present throughout the novel. His

fear of losing his clothes at the ball is a subconscious acknowledgement of his loss of manhood, one confirmed by
his actions at the ball. While unable to dance correctly with
Jane, he dances quite well with the cockney sailor when
forced to do so. Everything reinforces the impression that
Robert is not happily heterosexual, even the story of the
Japanese balloon which was a surrogate for a woman (194),
a misogynist's version of the mechanical nature of heterosexual relations.

The party climaxes in a riot. One man is set upon "like
a bear attacked by terriers from all sides" (195). Robert
witnesses a woman trying to ditch her drunken date in order
to keep another appointment, thereby confirming his
suspicion of human infidelity. The sordid party is climaxed for Robert by his rebuffing another attempted pickup by a male. To Robert, the entire party has epitomized
the condition of man: "Even the strange clothes had only
been the thinnest cloak over ordinariness and drabness;
there had been no job, no love, no pleasure, no delight and
no cohesion. Each little body had rushed about distractive-
ly, alone." (196). Only for a brief moment—when he was
dancing closely with the sailor—did Robert feel any rapport
with another human being. And for this reason the concept
of ordinary human pleasure filled him with utter despair.

After the ball, the remaining chapters are an anticlimax.
We are made privy to the observation that humans keep
pets only as emotional outlets for themselves, since human
contact is so unsatisfactory. We are told of a man who begs
another to tie him to the foot of his bed and to work his will
on him. And a final scene occurs in a churchyard of mauve
(again!) shadows, where a woman with red hair—clearly
representative of the life force—professes to love her dog
far more than she loves her baby.

Like A Voice Through a Cloud, the novel stands incomplete. But with scenes such as these, the message is clear:
man is always alone, isolated in a cruel and indifferent
universe without love. And, in his wretchedness, he per-
petuates cruel acts on others, making love even more impossible than before. The disappointment in mankind
which was registered in I Left My Grandfather's House is

here developed into nausea over the entire race. The references to Aubrey Beardsley and Oscar Wilde underscore the decadence. To give further point to his theme, Welch effectively borrowed from hearsay and legend, supersition and folklore. The novel contains some of his most overtly sexual writing, a fragment full of Krafft-Ebing, but nowhere does his craft decline. His descriptive powers, always acute, served him well here, and the pacing is quite swift.

CHAPTER 8

The Poems and
The Denton Welch Journals

I *Personal & Primitive*

THAT Denton Welch possessed a poetic eye there can be no doubt. His imagination was at times overburdened with its own inventiveness; when in great pain in the hospital, he asked himself, "Would the images never stop forming?"[1] To him, the crests of roofs in the snow looked "like the bones of big, rotting fishes, covered with salt." Carnations when carried bounced about "like cocks shaking their combs." Caviar was black and glistening as "oiled ball bearings." The sun sinking burned "to the ground like a red poker sinking into wood."

These are striking images, but they are not from Welch's poems. They were selected quite at random from the pages of *Maiden Voyage*, but other of Welch's prose works would have rewarded us with images just as poetic. This propensity makes it all the greater pity that Welch's poems—as poems—are so poor. In the total canon of sixty-seven poems collected in book form, there is only one image which I can compare with any of those just quoted; and it is found in "A Night Poem" in which Welch describes white orchids lying on a lady's hair as being "like gasping sailors in sick-bay." We can see the supine, floppy, white bell-bottomed limbs.

Surely Welch possessed the proper sensibility and technique to have become a competent poet. But he himself recognized his failures in that genre. In an exchange of letters with the poet Henry Treece (1912-1966), one of the leaders of the self-styled Apocalyptic movement, Welch admitted:

I agree with you in thinking that my poems are too narrowed down to one point. . . . And I also agree with you that they need attention. But here I must admit that however much I try, I still find it almost impossible to formulate to myself what I am *trying* to do when I write a poem. I just want to do it; and consequently what comes out of me will probably be rather shapeless, rather sexy and probably rather trite. My critical faculty, after the event, will tell me of these things, but it hasn't given me much help yet in remedying the faults."[2]

In another letter to Treece, Welch continued the self-criticism of his poetry: "I can't make out *what* is wrong with my poetry—something is. Do you think I'm really a prose writer? I have been writing poetry since I was nine years old, but I don't yet know what it's really all about. As a child I used to think that it was a rather pleasant magic process; but now I seem to have the greatest distaste for what I produce 'in that line.' "[3]

Remarks such as these indicate that Welch—always a fabulous original in his prose style, forging out *Maiden Voyage* as a very young man and under no real literary influence from anyone, for his Laurentian overtones came later—was at a loss when it came to poetic composition. For this reason I suggest he turned to another poet as model. It was not the work of either his adolescent idol, Robert Nichols, or his later friend and mentor Edith Sitwell that he turned to, though Dame Edith's rococo images and elegant rhythms and textures surely must have appealed to him. And it was not to the alliterative and curiously metrical poetry of Gerard Manley Hopkins, with whom Jocelyn Brooke seems to think Welch "felt an especial and intimate kinship."[4] Rather, it was a more austere model Welch chose: many of his poems seem to reveal an affinity for, and close reading of, A. E. Housman. And Welch acknowledges in his *Journals* the debt: "I have got a poetry bout on, but I keep on wondering if I'm producing semi-demi A. E. Housman. I should hate this, although he is a lovely poet. . . ."[5] Another entry records the fact that Welch had read all three of Housman's collections and also Laurence Housman's *Life* of the poet.

The attraction of Housman is understandable, not from a stylistic point of view, but from a consideration of subject matter. Welch shared Housman's love of life, his celebration of the pleasures of youth, his unacknowledged homosexuality, and his ultimate pessimism. Both wrote from a profound sense of personal loss in youth: for Housman it was his crushing academic failure which made him somewhat of a recluse for years; for Welch, his invalidism. Both writers were possessed by an unappeasable sadness. The numerous young farmers Welch described in his *Journal*, all unaware of impending fate, could well be the healthy Shropshire lads of Housman. Both Housman and Welch perceived the skull beneath the skin; both seem driven by their sense of the imminence of death to an attitude of *carpe diem*. The shadow of inexorable death falls across even so placid a poem of Housman's as "Loveliest of Trees." Rather than finding an objective correlative for death such as Housman's cherry trees, Welch was usually more direct: "Death is dangling his bait / And Greedy-Guts can hardly wait."

While Housman's subject matter and world view are compatible with Welch's, it is difficult to think that his unadorned and economic diction was. Housman's verse is a triumph of nouns and verbs; their powerful effect is achieved through the most sparing use of adverbs and adjectives. Welch's prose was heavily larded with both. In the first paragraph of *A Voice Through a Cloud*, for instance, the comb is described as ivory, then must be further modified as being "creamy-white." The protagonist's black bag is not just black, but "shiny black." Welch was forever elaborating on appearances; and, from a technical point of view, Housman was an odd exemplar for him. While Denton Welch was always somewhat of a renegade in his stories and novels, chronicling the unspeakable and the shocking, Housman was not even a "modern" poet. His extreme Englishness, his simplicity, and his lucidity were quite out of vogue in the post-*Waste Land* era.

Nowhere did Denton Welch's poems approach the achievement of Housman's lapidary lines. But from the older poet Welch seems to have learned lessons in control and reserve; and Welch was content to stop with these as his gleanings. Unlike Housman, he was unschooled in poetics; and he never really attempted to imitate the latter's metrical schemes

which were classic and regular. For the most part, Welch
wrote free verse, and occasionally employed rhyme. It is
only when his own voice falters and becomes an echo of
Housman's that we are reminded of the influence, as in
Welch's "Protection at Night," in which he begins the second
stanza with the invocation, "So let's still pass the whiskey
round,"[7] a line which invokes Housman's famous poem beginning "Think no more, lad; laugh, be jolly." Another
example of unassimilated Housman is Welch's verse titled
simply "Poem," which is quoted in its entirety:

> A few years back
> with drink and love
> 　　the rowdy boys were gay;
> But I sat still
> to wonder at
> 　　and watch their play.
>
> Now I am sad
> And long to catch
> 　　that bright, uprushing flame;
> But all the drinks
> Are drunk now
> 　　and the feet are lame.
> 　　　　　　　　(214)

There are, of course, many Housmanesque touches here,
the "rowdy boys," the use of drink as symbol for consumed
gaiety, the theme of youth's promise contrasted with its
continual betrayal. The poem of Housman's that Welch's
poem most immediately recalls, though by no means repeats,
is Number LIV from *A Shropshire Lad:*

> With rue my heart is laden
> 　　For golden friends I had,
> For many a rose-lipt maiden
> 　　And many a lightfoot lad.
>
> By brooks too broad for leaping
> 　　the lightfoot lads are laid;
> The rose-lipt girls are sleeping
> 　　in fields where roses fade.[8]

Both poets employ "lightfootedness" to personify youth. In Housman's poem the youths' leaping is terminated by death; in Welch's, by lameness. Spiritually, the result is the same.

There is much to admire in Welch's little poem. The poem's tact is actually superior to that of the Housman, for Welch does not tip his hand in the first stanza as does Housman, who tells the reader in the first two lines that the poet is sad because what once was is no longer. In the Welch poem, only in the second stanza does he admit, "Now I am sad." Further, there is an intriguing ambiguity about Welch's poem: are not the feet mentioned in the last line the narrator's own? Rather than the poet's sadness emanating from a realization that all his friends, once gay, are now old and crippled, perhaps the poet's biggest regret arises out of his own lameness, which now makes it impossible for him to participate in the pleasures which caution prevented him from sharing as a younger man. Whatever the application of Welch's regret, both the Welch and the Housman poems invite the reader by implication to seize the day, for each wasted day brings the inevitable closer.

Welch's "A Poem for Bathing" also falls within the same convention, and it has the same tone and pace of "With rue my heart is laden":

> My friends at the Y.M.C.A.
>   Dive into the glass-blue pool,
> And strike and splash and play
>   The gay light-hearted fool.
>
> But that is four years past,
>   Now only I remain;
> The others swam their last
>   Through mists of blood and pain.
>
> (222)

This poem reveals Welch's poetry at its best and its worst. His employment of the present tense in the first stanza is brilliant, causing a wrench in the reader when he arrives at the first line of the second stanza. And the sustained use of swimming imagery throughout, with the implied metaphor of life as a pool through which we must laboriously swim to the end, is successful. But Welch also is guilty of trite expression, especially in the infelicitous phrase, "And play the gay light-hearted fool."

Predictably this theme of lost youth occurs in his most Housman-like poems, those already discussed as well as "Protection at Night," "A Poem for the Future," "After Night Laughter," and "Stop Heart." The last poem almost paraphrases the second stanza of Housman's famous "Terence, This is Stupid Stuff," in which Housman proclaims, "Look into the pewter pot / To see the world as the world's not"—while Welch echoes, "Things don't appear the same / After so many beers." In numerous poems Welch draws the Housmanesque equation of youthful pleasure equaling beer drinking. One of the best of these is "A Poem for the Future," in which Welch's young men sing and dance atop a hill to celebrate the termination of military service and their survival of the war. Yet their joyous shouts are described as "empty." They are not empty in utterance, we feel, so much as empty to the poet's ears. Because the poet's ironic conclusion is that "all this noise because their Khaki's shed / So after all they'll live to die in bed." Welch is saying that we only exchange one mode of death for another; if not on the battlefield, we are destined to die in another way.

Lost youth is the theme of several of Welch's more original poems, too, such as "By the River" and the memorably imagistic "A Burst Love-Apple" in which a tomato symbolizes the ripeness of youth, which, like a tomato, must eventually spit out "its living jelly, scarlet jet, / Its spangled pepper-pot of seeds." Impermanence and loss of quite another kind are the subject of "Jane Allen," a poem which was published several times during Welch's lifetime and which has since been set to music by the composer Howard Ferguson. It is a poem in which a maid, described as a "fly-by-night," literally flies by night to her suicide. In only fifty words Welch gives us the character of the girl. She is so fastidious that, while her character may have been flighty, she still left the dishes "shining white" and darned the holes in her stockings before tending to what obviously must have been her preoccupation, her own suicide. The sound, pace,

and tone of the poem are carefully controlled so that the
reader shares the poet's surprise in discovering the note.
What seems a mere catalogue of chores accomplished ends
with the taking of her own life. In its understatement, the
poem is more moving than had Welch sentimentalized the
the deed.

But we must observe that none of Denton Welch's poems
is truly distinguished in the way that, say, his *A Voice
Through a Cloud* is. At their best, his poems could rank,
perhaps, with Lawrence's artificial verse in *Pansies* or with
some of Stephen Crane's sparsely poetic parables of *The
Black Riders*. Still, all of Welch's poems were not derivative
of Housman; and in those in which he was not concerned
with the inevitability of death (what he called in one inspired poem "the unchecked fox-trot of the years"), he poetically became more his own man. Some of these poems
are concerned with the themes of the senselessness of war,
man's inhumanity to man, lost love, and unfulfillment.
Many are ironic and are written in a highly colloquial
diction: "O then some moment from this stew / Must be
snatched out for me and you." While Welch has summoned
the word "stew" to connote the hopelessly confused state
of life, it also emphasizes, unfortunately, his unsuccessful
mastery of rhyme. To appreciate how wretched Welch could
be when attempting rhyme, we need only read his poem
"Scepticemia," in which for two stanzas every line ends in
an *a a a a* scheme, followed by a third stanza rhyming *aa bb
cc*: "As all truth / Has no ruth / So what is fine / Makes us
opine / That there is dirt / Beneath the white shirt." The
effect is comical rather than grave; the poem jangles along
like so much Ogden Nashery, rendering Welch into a rather
Melancholic Colley Cibber.

What redeems many of Welch's other poems, imbuing
them with a certain intrinsic interest despite their primitive
technique, is the infusion of his distinct personal vision—
so evident in his prose—into the verse. Unlike his Housman
imitations, many of the poems are almost Jacobean or Gothic
in their clutter of bodies and terrors, reminding us of the apparent Gothicism of *In Youth Is Pleasure*. Some are absolutely chilling, such as the innocently titled "You Never

Would Have Guessed," which is a monologue on infanticide; the "Fearful Dream," in which wax mannequins come alive and threaten the viewer's life; and "Awake," a poem which anticipates the situation of *A Voice Through a Cloud*, for a sick man lies awake at four o'clock in the morning in a hospital ward, studying "The bell that rings as a dumb wound screams." Throughout the poems, Welch's favorite images are coffins, bells, bones, bats, blood, earth, tombstones, violins, velvet, stagnant pools, the moon and the sea, the colors purple and black. The words "blood" and "bone" recur with maddening regularity, reminding us at once of his own fleshly affliction and his affinity for the Gothic novelists. These images are also linked to those in his pen-and-ink drawings, which are also full of bones and broken pediments, graphic presentations of the word-images of *In Youth Is Pleasure*. Maurice Cranston claims that such images "suggest the age of bogus ruins" and were "entirely authentic symbols for Denton Welch."[9] I suggest that it is not the bogus world's ruins which they conjure, but the body's ruins which Welch inhabited.

There is, for instance, a substantial body of poems on dead people, either soliloquies for the dead or to the dead. These include "For a Dead Conscript," "A Dead Man's Poem," "A Corpse's Poem," "For My Dead Sensualist," "Where Nothing Sleeps," "Parliament Square," "The Ship," and—one of his best—"For a Drowned Friend," in which the inconsequential nature of quotidian existence, synecdochized in "saving of brown paper and of string," is contrasted with the enormity of death.

War poems constitute another group. There is a keener awareness of the war raging around the writer in the poems than in any other of his writings save the *Journals* and certain stories in *A Last Sheaf*. In additon to "A Poem for the Future," already discussed, these include "Panacea," "Night in War-Time," "Rural Raid," and "For a Dead Conscript." Always a writer of domestic concerns, Welch nevertheless was inspired to some of his most effective imagery by the externalities of war. Lines such as the "oiled purr of bombers overhead" and "the sudden metal weight of fear" ring with authority. True, the war did not absorb him as it did Edith

Sitwell, who was humanized by it and produced after a de-
cade of poetic silence those essential war poems, of which
"The Canticle of the Rose," "Still Falls the Rain," and "The
Shadow of Cain" are not the least.

No, despite readings of Housman and the droppings of
bombs, Denton Welch's favorite subject remained Denton
Welch. But his treatment of Self differs in the poems from
the prose. His sexual conflict is not apparent from a reading
of the sixty-seven poems reprinted in *A Last Sheaf.* Unlike
his later novels and stories, in which the quest for experience and self-discovery was construed almost entirely in
sexual terms, sex is subjugated in the poems to other passions.
There is a tendency to intellectualize man, who in one poem
is called "The jelly-fish, whose soul has spread, until it earns
its daily bread" (232). Human sensuality is even found loathsome in "Easter Midnight Mass," in which the poet does
not wish to "drink from the cup / That so many other had
lifted up" (237). The contrast between his poems and his
prose is such that it almost seems that Denton Welch
thought sexual love and lust improper subjects for poetry,
that the genre demanded more elevated topics.

Because of these numerous limitations of technique and
attitude, the poems of Denton Welch do not constitute an
important part of his achievement. As works of art, they rank
evenly with his paintings, which also were arresting personal statements which were nowhere as original and successful as the best of his prose. Indeed, the best of his
poems recall his later paintings, which Dame Rose Macaulay
once described as "precise yet ghostly, like an odd and
beautiful and frightening dream."[10]

II *Revelation and Significance*

At the time of his death, Welch had seen through press
three books—*Maiden Voyage, In Youth Is Pleasure,* and
the stories in *Brave and Cruel.* He had all but completed the
novel *A Voice Through a Cloud,* and he had written several
new stories in the last year of his life. In 1952, the novel
was published; and it greatly enhanced his critical reputation; but the stories, gathered in *A Last Sheaf* (1951), did
not. Eventually a third posthumous book was felt important

enough to warrant publication by his editors and literary executor: *The Denton Welch Journals* (1952).

Taken from the notebooks which Welch kept for a good many of his productive years, it is a book which contains patches of some of his best writing. It also stands as a document of revelation and significance for anyone wishing to understand the man behind the books. Chronicling the life of the artist in close detail over a period of years, it is the kind of record of which far too few examples exist. Any journal represents years of reflection; but, as Cyril Connolly has observed, the journal of a sedentary writer like Welch represents an even greater challenge: confined to one place, condemned to monotomy, "the writer pits his mind, his privacy, the whole quality of his imagination against the reading public."[11] There can be, for instance, no fascinating travel sketches.

The *Journals* span the years 1942 to 1948. As published, the volume is a selective collection from all the entries recording Welch's adult life and personal experiences. The two editions so far available are not, unfortunately, the completely frank record which Welch put to paper. In his Introduction the editor, Jocelyn Brooke, admits to having found it "necessary to cut the manuscript of these journals down to a little over half its original length." While citing the law of libel as a primary reason for these deletions, the editor also admits that a number of the omitted passages, "though not legally actionable, might well have caused offence or embarrassment to the persons concerned. . . ."[12]

This is the risk one runs, of course, in publishing the diary of a man just dead. Yet it does seem regrettable that, in the second half of the twentieth century, a writer and his friends must be so "protected" by an editor. The reader is entitled to have his Welch the way it was written if he is to have it at all. The 1973 Hamish Hamilton edition of the *Journals* is but a reprint of the original version; no new material was added. While a number of these unpublished journal entries are said to be frankly homosexual by those who have read the manuscripts, other entries constitute the beginnings of short stories and novels. One of the most lengthy portions deleted by Mr. Brooke in his editing, the first chapters of the novel dealing with Welch's 1933 walking tour, fortunately has been privately printed since as *I Left My Grandfather's House* (1958).

What remains is a varied chronicle of Welch's life and personality, thoughts, and craft. They reveal a writer whose high professional standards toward his work never faltered, regardless of personal discomfort and, toward the end, knowledge of imminent death. The *Journals* also portray the writer at his most thoroughly unprofessional, disclosing the life of a high-strung, complex, temperamental young man who, in spite of obvious gifts, is visited with the full complement of human frailties, not the least of which were spitefulness, childishness, vanity, gloryseeking, and materialism.

He was also a snob (assessing one friend's background as having "a sort of trashy romance about it" (18); and he was callous, as far as his own family was concerned, his heart having held room for none but his mother (on his father's death he records, "it was really only the slightest shock and there was hardly any grief with it at all. . . . Would I be richer or poorer?" (25). Surprisingly, his compelling desire for fame was tempered by a realization of his limitations (capsulized in his wry verse, "O how I want to be great! / Delusion of grandeur's my fate" (1). Nevertheless, it becomes obvious at the outset of the *Journals* that Hell hath no fury like a Denton scorned; and it was one of his quirks to believe fairly regularly that he had been scorned by one party or another.

Regarded merely as a contribution to post-Bloomsbury literary history, *The Journals* would be of some consequence. There are lengthy impressions of Edith and Osbert Sitwell, Herbert Read, Harold Nicolson, Vita Sackville-West, Edward Sackville-West, and mentions of correspondence from E. M. Forster and Rose Macaulay, among others. Welch does not make many literary judgments of the work of these figures, however. (Indeed, he never wrote anything resembling literary criticism; he is probably one of the few literary figures of the past several decades who did not succumb to the writing of book reviews.) His judgments are reserved for the purely personal, the entries devoted to each constituting his version of the essence of Edith Sitwell or his personal impression of Herbert Read. As impressions they are strikingly written, as in his description of Dame Edith at the Sesame Club: "The tall figure dressed all in black, black trilby, Spanish witch's hat, black cloak, black satin dress to the ankles and two huge aquamarine rings. Wonderful rings on powder-white hands, and face so powder-pearly, nacreous white, almost not to be believed in, with the pinkened mouth, the thin, delicate, swordlike nose and tender-curling nostrils. No hair, I can remember no hair at first. The rings, the glistening satin, and the kid-white skin" (56).

But the *Journals* are more concerned with his own writing than with the facades, the lives, or the works of others. The reader readily discerns in the *Journals* an obsessive passion to produce a body of written work. Always at his back he heard time's winged chariot hurrying near. Even the *Journals* themselves, which began as a private diary during the days of pain, began to assume the form of a book which Welch fully intended to be published. As a book, the *Journals* possess more dramatic form than Welch perhaps could realize, beginning as the account does with his 1942 visit to Penshurst (Sidney's home) and ending with his 1948 visit to Sissinghurst (Vita Sackville-West's and Harold Nicolson's home). Even in his diary he was concerned with "voyages." The two trips are altogether different, however: the first is a small but lively party at which his first published piece was celebrated; the last, a social failure to which he had to be carried, so frail was his health. The form of the book is dramatic from another standpoint; it begins seemingly in midsentence ("And then we all met at Penshurst") and concludes with the breaking off in midsentence on page 268 ("Even now, as I write, I . . .").

Since the first volume of the *Journals* in manuscript is clearly labeled "Journal I," we can assume—as does Jocelyn Brooke—that the apparently disconnected first sentence was merely Welch's device for projecting the reader immediately *in medias res*. (We remember how abruptly some of the short stories seem to begin; "The Barn," for instance: "I turned and skidded obediently on the little path of lawn at the side of the house. . . .") The last sentence of the *Journals* is incomplete, of course, for reasons other than esthetic. But, by their very nature, all journals are fragmented and incomplete. Welch's is more than usually satisfying.

Nowhere in his writing did Welch more assiduously practice the cult of sincerity than in his journals. They record seven years of reflections on people, ideas, events, art, and, above all, himself. In their almost total commitment to self-revelation, *The Denton Welch Journals* have been compared by critics to W. N. P. Barbellion's *The Journal of a Disappointed Man* and to Ned Rorem's *Paris Diary*.[13] Cyril Connolly, reviewing Welch's journals in the London *Sunday Times*, was reminded of Katherine Mansfield's journal. And we know from Welch's own account that he had read Gide's journals; and we should mention *The Journal of Andre Gide* (though Welch lacked Gide's epigrammatical quality) and perhaps Virginia Woolf's *A Writer's Diary* as other obvious comparisons, despite the fact in its severely edited form, Mrs. Woolf's journal deals almost exclusively with the craft of fiction. Perhaps the best comparison, for its sheer John Clare-like freshness of insight and clarity of style, is to Francis Kilvert's *Diary.* He shared with Kilvert, whom he had read, the same vivid and splendid prose, the prose of Victorian "man of feeling"—as Horace Gregory has described Kilvert.

Welch devotes far less pages to comments on writing than does Virgina Woolf, but what he does say reveals a meticulous artist. We find that, with the exception of the entries in the *Journals* themselves, he created very slowly: "I am a snail worker turning out about four paragraphs a day and messing with my pictures till they are an obsession" (177). And once written, every piece was subjected to considerable rewriting, as was his practice from his first book forward. Commenting on the subsequent drafts of *Maiden Voyage,* he wrote: "I thought that to revise my first writing would only take a few weeks. I never dreamt that it was far the longest and most arduous part of the proceeding" (146). More than many, Welch realized the perspiration which must accompany inspiration if a successful work of art is to be realized. Lest some readers think the symbolic surface of Welch's writing accidental or unconscious, he defined writing as "stepping into the dark and making each tiny happening into a sign" (248). In his art, he was constantly erecting such signs.

Lady Oxford (later to become the Countess of Oxford and Asquith, with the given names of Emma Alice Margaret Asquith, but best known to Americans by her famous nickname, Margot, from publication of her witty *Autobiography of Margot Asquith* in 1922) once condemned Welch for the scene in *Maiden Voyage* in which a horse urinates, a rebuke he never understood or forgot. An integral part of his literary philosophy was to find meaning in the mean. He records the graffiti he once saw on a lavatory wall, and concludes, "It's all really poetry. . . . If the writers had more stamina and restraint it would be poetry. You must search the walls of public lavatories for heart-cries" (49).[14] Nearly everything he wrote incorporated an element of the sensational with a passion for minutiae. As a collector of antique miniatures who once spent months mending an eighteenth-century doll house (*Journals* 146-50), Welch also wrote about the seemingly small details of life which loomed large in his imagination. That is what he missed in reading the writers of the past: "I wish that people should mention the tiny things of their lives that give them pleasure or fear or wonder. I would like to hear the details of their houses, their meals and their possessions. I would like to hear the bits of family or intimate history they know" (141). We can imagine he was especially interested in their meals: Welch possessed a fearsome sweet-tooth; the boards binding the *Journals* groan from so many chocolates and jams.

While an omnivorous reader, Welch took little from those he read except in the case of his poetry, as we have demonstrated earlier in this chapter. In his prose—the genre he cared most about—he was determined to write about those subjects which interested him, however small or unconventional: "When I read about William Blake, I know what I am for. I must never be afraid of my foolishness, only of pretension. And whatever I have I must use, painting, poetry, prose—not proudly think it is not good enough and so lock it inside for fear of laughing, sneering" (159). Highly self-conscious, Welch had to walk the fine line between worrying what his readers would think if he wrote about what concerned him, and worrying about whether or not he really had anything to say:

I think that the murderous part of writing, the trying to force thought into a form that can be shared by others, is something that one shirks and turns away from with sick distaste in the morning, when it calls, and at night when one tries to have done with it. But it will never stop gnawing. There is always the longing to put the thoughts into the crude mincing machine. It is as if a madman were determined to make all the delicacies of a perfect music come through a brass trombone.

The other horror is that we are not rich enough, cannot take in all the thousand million things that we would have in every story. If we try, we only overload and are cumbersome.

All we can do is make a cheap little framework, that we hope is strong and resilient. (190)

Besides such proclamations about his art, the *Journals* are important to students because they contain many passages bearing the original remark, action, or character which Welch later transformed into fiction. The German prisoner, the woodcutter, the perpetual braggart, the dying mother, the invalid artist—all are here as embryonic art. It is fascinating to compare and contrast, to see just what Welch used from the raw material to shape his fiction. In most cases, he used everything available to him, and only then did he begin to elaborate.

Throughout the *Journals* book titles are strewn like dandelions in a field. The reader soon learns which books Welch admired and which he did not, and such knowledge conceivably could also be useful in assessing the shape of his own literary career and ouput. We learn, for example, that he greatly admired Joe Ackerley's *Hindoo Holiday*, which served as model for *Maiden Voyage*; but he disliked the stories of Somerset Maugham which Dame Edith had pressed upon him. He read and frequently quoted Horace Walpole, yet threw his copy of Wilde's *De Profundus* out the window, where it remained in sight but out of mind on an unreachable section of the roof. He loved the work of Gerard Manley Hopkins and A. E. Housman, but he did not admire the poems of Mr. Sigfried Sassoon. It is instructive that he was attracted more to nonfiction than to fiction, preferring biographies and autobiographies of writers and painters to novels—a taste which may be directly related to the strongly non-fictional flavor and aspects of his fiction. He records having read a life of the Brontes, Haydon's *Life*, Boswell's *Life of Johnson*, Montaigne, the letters of Gaudier-Brzeska, Gide's *Journal*, and others, including Francis Kilvert's *Diary* (1870-1879), which was published in three separate volumes in 1938, 1939, and 1940. The influence of Kilvert on Welch is yet to be explored; both were Divine Amateurs and remarkably spontaneous writers. The fiction he did read included Jane Austen, George Moore, Henry James, Aldous Huxley, Colette, and François Mauriac.

There are more literary than painterly books mentioned here, a contradiction of his usual interest in friends who were not from the world of letters but who tended to be either painters or, more often, not artistic at all. But the *Journals* reveal Welch was as happy to hear a red star had appeared on one of his paintings at the Leicester Gallery (indicating a sale) as he was when the postman brought an editor's letter of acceptance for a story or a poem.

Perhaps the most significant entry related to art explains Welch's individual technique for painting in oils, a technique he evolved in years of experimentation. He painted on mahogany boards, whitening the board first, then rubbing it down so that the mahogany showed through somewhat. Then the picture was outlined in pencil, and the outline was then carefully darkened with turpentine to strengthen the line. Then color was rubbed on very sparsely. The result pleased Welch, who described the technique as "direct, simple, permanent, and utterly unlike what is usually understood as oil painting" (36).

This reference is one of the few direct ones to his paintings that Welch made in the *Journals*. Just as his fiction was concerned with those day-to-day incidents which caught his fancy, so too was his diary. He rarely recorded dreams or fantasies, either, though his dream recounted on pages

256-57 combines his hatred of the desecration of churches with his fear of death; and the extraordinary dream of being cured and immediately offered a communion by a Prince Hamlet-Saviour-Friend figure is very interesting from a psychological viewpoint (241-43). No, his journals, as well as his fiction, were dedicated to the illumination of the commonplace. As John Lehmann has rightly observed, "His fantasy, curiously enough, seemed to go almost entirely into his exquisite little drawings and decorations, and the rare paintings of his mature style, so full of strange, poetic symbols."[15]

The *Journals* show just how great Welch's fascination with the commonplace really was. He possessed almost a *voyeur's* desire to "know" others, prompting him to perform such unusual acts as examining a used handkerchief found in a cossack hanging in an empty church vestry (75). In his encounters with muscular young men of the lower classes, his curiosity was especially great. Welch was romantically enchanted by working-class males, whose lives, experiences, interests, and even physiques were different from his.

Slight and disabled, Welch's adult life was an embarkment upon an imaginative search for the Ideal physique — the ectomorph seeking the mesomorph. The *Journals* contain numerous descriptions of the very physical types — those Laurentian-Housmanesque heroes — that Welch encountered and detained on his walks, young men whose beauty impressed him sufficiently to compel him to describe them on paper at length when he returned home. He was frank about this predilection, at least insofar as he acknowledged that he possessed a capacity for "hero-worship" of the extremely masculine, those who were all he was not, "stalwart, confident, and settled into a 'manly' life" (31).[16]

Whatever pleasure Welch derived from these chance encounters — sunbathing with a farmhand, sharing chocolates with a soldier — was always tempered by his awareness of the ephemeral nature of youth and beauty and even of health (see his poem "The Demon Soul" (51). After one such encounter, he apostrophized, "Now, stranger, whose name I have quite forgotten — where are you now? Even if you are not dead in battle, that 'You' is dead and nowhere, for at most it could only have lasted a year or two—that animal magic" (33). After another he wrote: " 'Good luck,' I said heartily, thinking to myself, We'll never see each other again, we'll both grow older and older and uglier and uglier; the earth will bloom, the hops bristle and curl, when we'll both be too disgusting to think of" (78).

This search for an Ideal culminated in his friendship with Eric Oliver, and the *Journals* make clear the contrasts between Eric's free and pub-crawling life and Welch's drawing-room existence. As presented in the *Journals*, their relationship often bordered on that of father and son. However interpreted, it was at once Welch's salvation and frustration. On the basis of Welch's own accounts, there can be no doubt of Mr. Oliver's infinite patience and kindness toward the ailing writer, or of the importance Welch placed on his friendship. At the same time, Welch frequently longed to be left totally alone to think and create in what time was left him. Despite differences, Eric Oliver seems to have filled a great need in Welch's last years. Welch, who saw his own life as split into two great periods, wrote of them thusly: "Accident and Illness" and "Love and Friendship." Eric Oliver's advent was as positive as Welch's accident was negative.

Outside his journals, Welch never wrote about his friendship with Eric Oliver. And there is other material here which he also might have transformed into fiction, had he lived. Certainly the episode of the Old Boy's return to Repton on Speech Day (40-44) would have made an excellent short story; in its present form in the *Journals*, it already reverberates with ambiguities of innocence and knowledge, and recalls in theme and situation Welch's well-turned story, "When I Was Thirteen." While Welch was always an astute judge of character, the study of Miss Wigan of Luddesdown Church is especially fine (212-17), and constitutes one of the few lengthy accounts of a woman in the journal save that of Edith Sitwell.

Aside from his work, working-class men, and descriptions of his illness (which are bettered in *A Voice Through a Cloud*), the *Journals* are given over to his preoccupation with antiques and architecture. Some of his happiest accounts are of rummaging in antique and junk shops and making a "find." A true artist, his urge to create extended to his shaping his immediate environment. He felt compelled to surround himself with what he considered beautiful—recalling Wallace Steven's pronouncement, "I am what is around me." About architecture, Welch was outspoken; and some entries ramble to great length describing details of the latest ancient church he has visited. Throughout the *Journals*, Welch conveys a sense of the English landscape being spoiled by man, with the tearing down of old churches, the cutting down of stately stands of trees. His expressed desire to build a tower and live in it forever (82) or to live on a wild heath like the Brontes (74) indicates how total his alienation was from that life which passed for reality which surrounded him.

Taken as a whole, *The Denton Welch Journals* is one man's direct response to life. Like Gide, Welch used his journals for rapid writing, making no revisions, saving precious hours for revising what he considered his more important work. The result of such spontaneous creation is prose of an unusual purity and freshness, with no pretenses or personae assumed. The pages yield a vividness produced from enthusiasm. What unfolds is the life of a suffering young man which is tragic but never pathetic. Denton Welch made the most of what talent and time he had, and how many of us can say the same?

CHAPTER 9

Reputation and Contribution

I *Limitation*

WHEN Welch died at the age of thirty-three, his friends and admirers spoke of the great loss to English literature. Edith Sitwell, for instance, wrote John Lehmann from the Hotel St. Regis, New York, on hearing the news: "Poor little Denton, I am filled with sadness about him. Not thirty [*sic*] and so gifted as a prose writer."[1] But today more than twenty years after his death, we must ask, How great was this loss? One critic, in reviewing Welch's second novel, has compared the excitement which greeted Welch's virtuosity with that provoked by the early novels of Aldous Huxley and Richard Hughes. He thought Welch an extraordinarily capable young English writer who would help revitalize the craft of fiction.[2] Welch hardly went on to do that. In his lifetime, his talent already began to be devalued; and in January, 1949, a week after Welch's death, the anonymous reviewer of *Brave and Cruel*—unaware of Welch's passing—declared in the *London Times* that "if Mr. Welch can remain severely objective, he has talent to be developed." The substance of this ironic evaluation must be considered.

The critics are in disagreement even today. In 1966, John Updike suggested that Welch's gifts, "liberated to wider use by a healthy life, would have proved equal to vast subjects," and that, possibly, "save for his accident he would have outgrown the distrustful and diffident brilliance of a schoolboy."[3] But John Lehmann, on the other hand, believes Welch's art would not have grown had he lived. Welch once confided to Lehmann that he always felt obliged to record events with exact accuracy; and, according to Lehmann, "he was always up against the problem of accomodating the artistically feasible to this strict conscience about his own experience. Even when writing in the third person, he admitted to me, it made little or no difference." Lehmann concludes that, for this reason, he wonders if Welch could have gone on writing fiction at all. He envisions him, instead, as "developing into the most disconcerting diarist of our day; an English Gide, but a more delicate and exotic bird. . . ."[4]

Welch confessed to others that he could be nothing but honest, even about the unconventionalities of his life. In an extraordinary letter to the Midlands poet Henry Treece he declared:

It really has been horribly difficult, all through childhood and adolescence, resisting the jokes and prods of parents, guardians, brothers and even friends; and now that I am independent I absolutely refuse to cloak what transparency and honesty remain to me in the conventional cloaks of heartiness, sophistication, irony, and satire, which most people seem to find so very useful.

I am conscious of the embarrassing qualities of my stories (so easy to guy effectively) but it would be dishonest of me to write in a more adroit and worldly-wise way. Perhaps it is wrongheaded of me to write of what I do, as I do, at this particular moment in the world's history, but it is certainly not mere frivolity or exhibitionism that prompts me. If this were the case, the embarrassments, difficulties, and misunderstandings caused by *Maiden Voyage* alone, would have cured me long ago. I am quite prepared to make myself appear ridiculous if in the process I gain experience as a writer. This is the thing I want most.[5]

Such refusal to compromise facts and to fictionalize life no doubt is part of the reason Welch's books were not more widely appreciated in his time: no one was certain whether they were fiction or autobiography! As novels, their form is usually unsatisfactory. Most have no "conclusion" at all (the exception being *In Youth Is Pleasure*). He handled subsidiary characters clumsily. But today, in an age of Truman Capote's "nonfiction novel" and Norman Mailer's "history as a novel, the novel as history," we surely can be more receptive to Welch's highly personalized approach to fiction. Ruby Cohn has admirably demonstrated that those of Welch's volumes most likely to be labeled autobiographical because of subject *(Maiden Voyage* and *A Voice Through a Cloud)* can be "singularly instructive to students of the contemporary novel" in matters of form and technique.[6] Cohn is right to say what is especially admirable is Welch's deliberate juxtaposition of the important and the trivial, his choice of dramatic events, and his understated conclusions.

Another reason Welch is not accorded greater recognition is the narrowness of his range. He did not, like a Balzac, a Proust, or a Faulkner, populate an entire imaginative landscape and society. Instead, in book after book, story after story, he gave us the only real character he could present: Denton Welch. He was, in Maurice Cranston's words, "a born solipsist, who expected Nature to hold the mirror up to him." Of course—the artist is by definition a solipsist. Friends and family were mere shadow figures, shunted on and off stage at the author's convenience, disappearing as soon as he lost interest in them. He eschewed scenic descriptions, plots, motivations, climaxes, and epiphanies (except in a few of the short stories) in favor of a more personal, anecdotal narrative line in which, as W.H. Auden observed, the Ego is narrator rather than the Self.

But Auden also has spoken of Welch's "combination of scientific objectivity with subjective terror" as contributing to his writings' "revealing comment on our historical situation."[8] Surely the subjectivity and terror are there; but what comment on historical or topical situations does Welch make? That lack is one of the very limitations of his work. It is so highly subjective that the sensibility is the total resource, for his stories exist outside time and space, like fairy tales. More than one critic has noted that his work did not reflect the aggressions of a world at war, that Welch did not connect the internal with the external world. His personal dilemmas rarely are given social dimension (except in *A Voice Through a Cloud,* which is one reason that work remains his most "meaningful" book). Too often his world is a private rather than a universal one. In many of the stories, and in *In Youth Is Pleasure,* the reader does not gain a sense of Welch's time and place and experience— England during World War II.

We must not, however, overstress th's supposed "limitation." As his letter to Henry Treece reveals, Welch was aware that his works were totally unhistc ical. He was committed to creating works of "pure art," and those who would dismiss them as totally "divorced from life" are assuming nothing is worth writing about except a particular, prescribed world-outlook. Such critics would, by extension, have also to dismiss such pure love stories as *Romeo and Juliet,* Turgenev's *Torrents of Spring,* or *Manon Lescaut.* Such readers ultimately would dismiss any and all writers who do not directly concern themselves with contemporary affairs, or who do not think of men as masses (a nation, a race, an economic class) instead of individuals. Welch was concerned with his individual psyche, and I maintain that every man's intimate history is universal history. Ontogeny recapitulates phylogeny.

Yet because it always was Welch's own story which he had to tell, and none other, critics (Dame Edith Sitwell among them) accused Welch of suffering from the ingrown toenail, with everything growing inward. Maurice Cranston stated, "If he could have seen the wider human comedy with his miraculously penetrating vision, and described that world as he described his own, he would assuredly have been among the greater writers in our language." Instead, Cranston concludes, "he will survive as a miniature genius, one of the very few from an uncreative age."[9] Fortunately, others who have found this restriction of vision a virtue have concluded that Welch produced work which must be accepted as fiction of the first rank, and if the novels are psychological casebooks rather than "pure" fiction, as Walter Allen maintains, they nevertheless are "the casebooks of a writer who was touched with genius,"[10] a view also held by Alan Pryce-Jones. Pryce-Jones found in Welch "a radiant air of telling the truth inseparable from the act of standing back a little, as if in order to see better. The truth of Denton Welch is a visionary truth, the vision wears a personal color which stains everything upon which it falls."

He categorizes Welch's *oeuvre* with Harold Nicolson's *Some People*,—books in which the autobiographer found it easier to talk about himself obliquely—"not in the manner of Henry Adams, but under the disguise of fiction."[11] Pryce-Jones reaches Lehmann's conclusion, however, when he states that, because Welch gave us in so little time so much that was both particular and complete, "had Welch lived to be 70, he could scarcely have added to the denseness and clarity which made him so memorable a writer."[12]

We do have to wonder what, given Welch's artistic credo, he could have written next. He had explored his childhood in *Brave and Cruel*, adolescence in *Maiden Voyage*, college years in the unfinished novel of *A Last Sheaf*, and the invalidism which was to be his adult life in *A Voice Through A Cloud*. It could perhaps be said that his death spared him artistic frustration as well as an extremely painful old age. He had already told his life story as best as he could tell it.

II *Achievement*

Accepting the corpus of his work as complete despite early death, what then are Denton Welch's achievements? First, he forged an admirable prose style, one which is seldom surpassed in our time for sheer beauty. This young man, whose formal academic education ended with the last year of preparatory school, commanded a language that was "tight and hard and sure and incisive and clean as a fresh wind blowing,"[13] as the many quotations in the body of this study should reveal. Through his omnivorous reading and his artist's eye, Welch became a master of prose, not in the convoluted style of James or Faulkner or Elizabeth Bowen, but rather in the supremely lucid manner of imagistic poetry, or prose pared of all excess, such as found in the diaries of Francis Kilvert. The beauty of Welch's imagery was not all wind and silver. Cyril Connolly crystallized Welch's writing in this way: "Disease was ever present, and the shadow of death, as if conscious of the meaningless cruelty to which they had condemned him, mitigated his fate by sharpening his gifts of clarity, intuition, an unfailing effortless liaison with the right words. One is never conscious of hard work and erasures: his style ripens like an

October pear that measures every hour of sunshine against the inevitable frost."[4]

Welch's style is rich, but, contrary to the claims of some, it is not really precious. Preciousness (according to Anais Nin, who ought to know) "is an elaboration which is not essential to meaning." Richness, on the other hand, "is what is essential to the meaning, texture, mood, atmosphere, rhythm, and color."[15] Welch needed such richness to convey the world of his imagination. The language of action can be simple and direct; but the language of sensation, emotion, intuition, and instinct—everything which concerned Denton Welch—cannot be.

Second, despite the fact that Welch seemed nearly a solipsist, he was able to render his preoccupations with lost innocence, individuality, youthful and adolescent fears, sexual frustrations and the transitoriness of life into works of art which are universal. Denton Welch succeeded in speaking the unspeakable with detachment and candor. His vision, sometimes Kafkaesque, is meaningful in the era of the H-bomb and the Inter-Continental Ballistic Missile, even though such threats go unnamed. It is Kafkaesque with its helpless and innocent protagonist loose in a world gone wrong, and it is Laurentian in the protagonist's affirmations of individuality. Although as contemporary as Kafka, Welch, as we have demonstrated, invites certain conceptual comparisons with those other universal artists, Dante and Chaucer. His influences were Lawrence, Housman, and the Gothic novelists, but his style was ultimately his own.

It is doubtful that Welch's fiction has been a creditable influence upon any writer currently of note. His style and vision were too individual to be of direct use by others. His formless, open-ended fiction can be seen, however, as interesting antecedents of the more revolutionary artistic products of the 1960's, such as the experimental stories of John Barth (*Lost in the Funhouse*), the films of John Cassavetes (*Husbands*) and the novel of Andy Warhol (*A*). As our discussion of *I Left My Grandfather's House* reveals, Welch's writing can be compared to such picaresque models as Bunyan; and today *Maiden Voyage* seems one of

the first in the revival of the English picaresque, a movement which later gained fame through the "Angry Young
Man" novels of John Wain, Philip Larkin, Kingsley Amis
(Lucky Jim), and Iris Murdoch *(Under the Net)*, as well
as through the plays of John Osborne. The exquisitely con-
ceived, dramatically developed novel of intelligence as
practiced by Henry James and followed by legions was
abandoned, more or less at midcentury, for the more chaotic,
"existential" novel of the picaresque. (We use here the
popularized conception of existential, meaning "not knowing what will happen next.") We must not rush to give Welch
much—if any—credit for this movement toward the picaresque, however. After all, *Tristam Shandy* is highly picaresque, too, and could be called quite existential; and it
was published in 1760.

More appropriately, *A Voice Through a Cloud* belongs
in the company of that small body of French novels produced
by writers influenced by the German existentialist philosophers Edmund Husserl, Martin Heidegger, and Karl
Jaspers. I am thinking particularly of the novels of Jean-
Paul Sartre and Albert Camus. There is no evidence from
his journals or letters that Welch studied these philosophers
or read any of these novels. Yet if comparisons are to be
made at all, in its acceptance of the "absurdity" of the world
of reality, *A Voice Through a Cloud,* published in 1950, is
clearly in the tradition of Sartre's *Nausea* (1938) and Camus's
The Stranger (1942). Welch's book could be included with
them in any course in twentieth-century existential novels.

Welch's protagonist, Maurice, whose body through an
accident has become "grotesque," is a soul-mate of Sartre's
Roquentin, who also finds himself alienated from his own
body, and whose struggle against "nausea" culminates in
his acceptance of it as the essential truth of life. For both
Maurice and Roquentin, the veneer of life has been peeled
away to reveal (in Sartre's words) the "frightful, obscene
nakedness" underneath.

With his constant setbacks and relapses, Maurice is also
like the figure in the Greek myth of Sisyphus, who was condemned by the gods to endlessly roll a heavy boulder up a
hill, only to have it roll down and the process begin again.

Sisyphus was the type of the hero in the world of Camus'
imagination; the French writer took the fable's futility as a
figure for the absurdity of all life and the endlessness of
trial (see *The Myth of Sisyphus*, 1940). This is a view Welch's
protagonist is forced to share. We recall the ball of wool
which Maurice endlessly winds and unwinds, his Sisyphian stone. Maurice concludes, "Now I knew nothing
was real but pain, heat, blood, tingling, loneliness, and
sweat" (23). Like Camus and Sartre, Welch considered
suicide as a serious answer to the problem of life's absurdity,
but ultimately he argued against it.

Welch's novel more closely resembles Sartre's in its
realism, its root in the things of this world. Camus' spare
fictions (*The Stranger; The Plague; The Fall*) are more overtly
didactic, for situations are contrived to register a point.
However, Welch does share with Camus the opinion that
to scorn our absurd, Sisyphian existence is to transcend it.
As Camus' Caligula says in the play bearing his name,
"The world has no importance. Once he realizes that a
man wins his freedom." Welch's Maurice even reaches
the point where he can gloat about the horror of his situation
and surroundings. When he returns to the nursing home
with Dr. Farley, he is "filled with this sense of the absurdity
of everything on earth. Nothing was fixed and sure. We all
melted into ridiculousness in the end" (154). Maurice sees
human intercourse as "impertinent and ludicrous" (218)
and acknowledges his own callousness to Self and to others
as Truth. Like Camus' Meursault (of *The Stranger*), he
experiences the world's indifference to humans; and he,
in his own indifference, has penetrated to the secret of
reality, a vision also set forth in Camus' *The Plague:* "In
this extremity of solitude, none could count on any help
from his neighbor; each had to bear the load of his troubles
alone."

Maurice in his plight, beset by accident and illness, is a
figure for man's fate in a meaningless world. Welch's vision
of impotence in *A Voice Through a Cloud* is a potent
existential document, and this is perhaps the difference
between Welch's last (and best) novel and other more
famous novels about the coming-of-age. Welch had developed

from the traditional writer of an apparently autobiographical novel, *Maiden Voyage*—which in thematic respects is comparable to Bennett's *Clayhanger* or Maugham's *Of Human Bondage*—to an unconventional, existentialist one. While none of Welch's writing is detached—the reader is always close to the protagonist, Welch is always engaged with him —nevertheless, by the time he came to write his last novel, he was more concerned with the inner human condition than with the outer worldly encounters. He seems to have come to share, with D. H. Lawrence, Dorothy Richardson, and James Joyce, the knowledge that reality lies in labyrinthine complexity beneath the surface of things. By definition, his reality had to embrace the unseen as well as the seen, the intuited as well as the experienced. Yet, despite this link with Joyce, Maurice could never think of exclaiming (as Joyce's Stephen), "Welcome, O life! I go to encounter for the millionth time the reality of experience and to forge in the smithy of my soul the uncreated conscience of my race." Because for Maurice the uncreated conscience is not worth creating, the reality of experience is nothing more than nothingness. With its helpless hero and its recreation of the world of pain, Welch's novel must be considered an existentialist creation of some importance. Its subject and vision are more comparable to the Book of Job and to Irishman Smauel Beckett's *Molloy* trilogy, as well a to the French authors cited, than to any English picaresque or *bildungsroman*.

Another link with the French, that to the French Objectivists, has been noted by critic Ruby Cohn. Professor Cohn sees Welch as anticipating that movement.[16] However, the Objectivist poets, such as William Carlos Williams and Wallace Stevens in this country, select material objects for study and presentation for their own particular value as objects rather than for their ability to symbolize an emotion or an intellectual concept of the poet. I hope I have shown that Welch, if he resembles any school of poets, was more a Symbolist with his clusters of images and metaphors that suggest the basic emotions behind his work. In the words of Jean-Paul Sartre, Welch's compositions are "inhabited by a soul, and since there must have been motives, even hidden ones, for the painter [substitute writer] to have chosen yellow rather than violet, it may be asserted that the objects thus created reflect his deepest tendencies."[17]

In the genre of poetry, perhaps Welch's work could more appropriately be said to be a literary antecedent of today's "confessional" poets—those highly subjective writers whose work is an expression of personality, not an escape from it; whose work is therapeutic or purgative; displays moral courage; and uses the Self as a poetic symbol. Like Welch's novels, the work of these poets—Allen Ginsberg, Robert Lowell, Sylvia Plath, Anne Sexton, John Berryman —portrays the alienated and afflicted Self in poetic terms. But, unlike these latter-day confessors, Welch erected certain barriers between himself and the reader. On matters of sex, he was never entirely open. He had, moreover, greater interest in evocative language than in the open, flat language of ordinary speech of a Ginsberg or a Plath.

Despite these real and alleged links, Denton Welch will be remembered for his individual voice and terrible vision rather than as the progenitor or member of any literary movement or school. In his very individuality and prolif-icness he fulfilled his destiny. I have called his life "Christ-like," but not because he suffered an early death on a cross of pain. Christ's injunction to take up the cross and follow him is not a literal one in which the individual is to reenact the drama of His life—not the literal Imitation of Christ, which has been the delusion of Western man in his search for the historical Jesus. In fact, the basis of Western Civil-ization can be said to be founded on a fundamental error, the mistaken notion of self-sacrifice as martyrdom, when Christ meant in truth that the individual must fulfill his own unique destiny. In the case of Christ, this destiny happened to culminate in the Crucifixion. (In the true, Hebraic sense in which Jesus understood sacrifice, to sacrifice oneself is not to deny one's Self, but to "draw near" to God.) In the case of Denton Welch, fulfillment meant the completion of his life-work, which he truly accomplished. He had produced as much in his brief writing career as some do in a lifetime.

With *A Voice Through a Cloud,* it was finished. He had done the work he was meant to do.

For that we can be grateful. Few modern writers reward the reader with such visual delights. Not many have written as memorable a book as *A Voice Through a Cloud.* If Welch is repetitive and restrictive, so too are the masters; how many different times and in how many different ways did Henry James write the same "international" novel? As Marcel Proust sensed, "The great men of letters have never created more than a single work, or rather have never done more than refract through various mediums an identical beauty which they bring into the world."[18]

Notes and References

Chapter One

1. Details for this biographical portrait are taken from the memoirs of Helen Roeder, Hector Bolitho, and Maurice Cranston; correspondence from Eric Oliver to Robert Phillips; and a letter of April, 1945, from Denton Welch to Peggy Kirkaldy.

2. Marcel Proust, *Jean Santeuil* (New York, 1955), p. 31.

3. For these and many other facts in the following account I am indebted to an undated autobiographical fragment and to letters by Denton Welch that are housed in The Academic Center Library, University of Texas.

4. Letter from Welch to a Miss Cooper, Oct. 29, 1943.

5. Autobiographical fragment.

6. See Eric Oliver, Introduction, *A Last Sheaf* (London 1951), p. 7.

7. *Ibid.*

8. Autobiographical fragment.

9. *Brave and Cruel* (London, 1948), p. 54.

10. Jocelyn Brooke, "Introduction," *Denton Welch. Extracts from His Published Works* (London, 1963), p. viii.

11. Autobiographical fragment.

12. *The Denton Welch Journals*, ed. Jocelyn Brooke (London, 1952), p. 4.

13. *Denton Welch. Extracts from His Published Works*, p. ix.

14. *Ibid.*, p. x.

15. Letter from Welch to Alex Comfort, dated Jan. 5, 1943.

16. Letter from Welch to Basil Jonzen, June 16, 1943.

17. Letter from Welch to Maurice Cranston, Aug. 24, 1942.

18. Helen Roeder, "Ariel in the Tree Trunk," *I Left My Grandfather's House* (London, 1958), n.p.

19. *Ibid.*

20. *A Voice Through a Cloud* (London, 1951), 118.

21. *The Denton Welch Journals*, p. 34.

22. *Ibid.*, p. 113.

23. Noel Adeney, *No Coward Soul* (London, 1956), p. 53.

24. *Journals*, p. 160.

25. *Ibid.*, p. 155.

26. See Welch's account of this meeting in the *Journals*, pp. 10-15.

27. Letter from Denton Welch to Alex Comfort, Jan. 5, 1943.

28. Constantine FitzGibbon, *The Life of Dylan Thomas* (Boston, 1965), pp. 177-78, 194-95.

29. Letter from Welch to Betty Swanwick, May 12, 1943.

30. Letter from Edith Sitwell to Denton Welch, May 2, 1945.

31. Quoted in the second volume of Lehmann's autobiography, *I Am My Brother* (New York, 1960), p. 242.

32. Letter to Helen Roeder, April 2, 1943.

33. Frank Swinnerton, *Figures in the Foreground* (New York, 1964), p. 234.

34. Helen Roeder, "Ariel in the Tree Trunk," n.p.

35. Letter to Henry Treece, June 9, 1943.

36. This was not an uncommon London editorial practice in the first third of the century. Alex Waugh tells how the publisher Duckworth wanted Evelyn Waugh to change the supposedly shocking portions describing schoolboy hazing in *Decline and Fall*. There seemed to be a gentlemen's agreement that public schools were sacrosanct. Alec Waugh, *My Brother Evelyn and Other Portraits* (New York, 1967), p. 181.

37. Letter from Welch to the Rev. Peter Gamble, Jan. 20, 1944.

38. *Journals*, p. 82.

39. Letter from Welch to Eric Oliver, July 4, 1944.

40. Letter from Eric Oliver to Robert Phillips, June 22, 1967.

41. *No Coward Soul*, p. 148.

42. Maurice Cranston, "Denton Welch," *The Nineteenth Century and After* (Oct., 1950), p. 238.

43. Letter from Welch to Peggy Kirkaldy, Oct. 25, 1945. The recipient was a woman who lived in a country home in Essex and who was an avid and overawed fan of at least two literary figures of the period, Denton Welch and Dorothy Richardson. She was most generous with her time, sending Welch books and objects. Welch responded with very warm and grateful letters, as did Miss Richardson. Horace Gregory has identified Peggy Kirkaldy as a member of London's "non-philistine middle class, that held conservative opinions yet delighted in venturing near the fringes of art and bohemia." Gregory, who has read the large collection of Dorothy Richardson's letters in the Yale University Library, considers the correspondence received by Peggy Kirkaldy

to be, along with those to Henry Savage, the best of Dorothy Richardson's many letters. The same could be said of the letters she occasioned from Welch. See Gregory's *Dorothy Richardson: An Adventure in Self-Discovery* (New York, 1967), pp. 7-14.

44. Letter from Welch to Peggy Kirkaldy, Aug. 15, 1946.

45. Letter from Edith Sitwell to Denton Welch, May 2, 1945.

46. *Journals*, p. 196.

47. Hector Bolitho, "My Friendship with Denton Welch," *Texas Quarterly* (Winter 1967), pp. 235-41.

48. Noel Adeney, *No Coward Soul*, p. 185.

49. Eric Oliver, Foreword, *A Voice Through a Cloud*, p. v.

50. The book's title was chosen by John Lehmann, its publisher, after Welch's death. See Lehmann's *The Ample Proposition* (London, 1966), pp. 116-18.

51. Letter to Peggy Kirkaldy, Nov. 21, 1948.

52. Eric Oliver, Foreword, *A Voice Through a Cloud*, p. v.

53. John Lehmann, *The Ample Proposition*, p. 118.

Chapter Two

1. William Matthews, *British Autobiographies Before 1951* (Berkeley, 1955).

2. Herbert Read, "Surrealism and the Romantic Principle," in *Criticism*, ed. Mark Schorer, Josephine Miles, and Gordon McKenzie (New York, 1958), p. 108.

3. As quoted by Richard Chase, *The American Novel and Its Tradition* (New York, 1957), p. 26.

4. Isabella Athey, "A Boy's Life," *The Nation* (April 21, 1945), pp. 462-64.

5. All page references are to the original American edition published by L. B. Fischer (New York, 1945).

6. Frederick R. Karl implies the book's title is derived from the protagonist's tender transvestite yearnings, *The Contemporary English Novel* (New York, 1962), p. 287.

7. For a full discussion of this psychological condition of aggression and the constant need for oral gratification, the reader is referred to "Fantasies and Dreams in Schizophrenia" by Geza Roheim, in his posthumously published study *Magic and Schizophrenia* (Bloomington, Indiana; 1955), pp. 93-227.

8. Joseph Campbell, *The Hero With a Thousand Faces* (New York, 1956), 245-46. See also p. 30.

9. Campbell, p. 58.

10. Campbell, p. 123.

11. See C. G. Jung, *Psyche & Symbol* (New York, 1958), p. 175.

12. See Otto Rank, *The Myth of The Birth of The Hero* (New York, 1959).

13. Welch appears to have adopted this alchemical notion for his own in his art. See the discussion of his painting of the beaker of urine in *A Voice Through a Cloud* in Chapter 5 of this study.

14. Campbell, p. 92.

15. C. G. Jung, "The Phenomenology of the Spirit in Fairy Tales," *The Archetypes and the Collective Unconscious*, tr. R. F. C. Hall. Second edition, The Collected Works of C. G. Jung, Vol. IX, Part I. (Princeton, 1968), p. 223.

16. C. G. Jung, "Christ, A Symbol of the Self," *Aion. Researches Into the Phenomenology of the Self*, tr. by R. F. C. Hall. The Collected Works of C. G. Jung, Vol. IX, Part II. (Princeton, 1959), pp. 36-72.

17. *Ibid.*, p. 40.

Chapter Three

1. Maurice Cranston, "Denton Welch," *English Critical Essays*, Twentieth Century, Second Series, ed. Derek Hudson (London, 1958).

2. Hamilton Basso, "Bread" *The New Yorker*, XXII (April 6, 1946), 106-08.

3. Identified by Jocelyn Brooke as the Oatlands Park Hotel, near Weybridge, in his introduction to *Denton Welch. A Selection* (London, 1963). Welch also discusses the Oatlands site in his journals. See page 258.

4. Cranston, "Denton Welch," *English Critical Essays*, Twentieth Century, Second Series, p. 336.

5. Page references are to the American edition (New York: L. B. Fischer, 1946).

6. See Note 218 to "The Waste Land," *T. S. Eliot. The Complete Poems and Plays, 1909-1960* (New York, 1962), p. 52.

7. Like Algernon Charles Swinburne, Denton Welch probably carried into his adult life certain strong memories of public school floggings which later manifested themselves in his work. With Swinburne, of course, the recollections became obsessions. We need not know if Welch himself had masochistic instincts during boyhood, but in his recollections of boyhood they do seem to prevail. This masochism perhaps was a development of his later life, when he was physically and sexually incapacitated. It is significant that his most sacred memory of his mother in *In Youth Is Pleasure* is of her beating him with the bristly side of her hair brush!

Chapter Four

1. Eric Oliver, "Foreword," A *Voice Through a Cloud*. London, 1951, p. v.

2. Jocelyn Brooke, "Introduction," *Denton Welch. Extracts From His Published Works* (London, 1963), p. xxv.

3. *Brave and Cruel and Other Stories* (London, 1948), p. 7. Citations refer to the book as issued by Star Editions Ltd., London.

4. C. E. M. Joad, *Decadence: A Philophical Inquiry* (London, 1948), pp. 290-93.

5. For a brief summarization of Charon's function, see Edith Hamilton's *Mythology* (New York, 1940), pp. 39, 227-28.

6. In America, the story is currently available in at least two popular anthologies: The Vintage paperback *23 Modern Stories*, edited by Barbara Howes (New York, 1963); and World Publishing Company's *Rite of Becoming*, edited by Arthur and Hilda Waldhorn (New York, 1966).

7. Basil Davenport, "What Will Become of Orvil Pym?" *Saturday Review*, XXIX (June 22, 1946), 24.

8. See Wilhelm Stekel's "Representation of Parapathy in Dreams," *Zentralblatt für Psychoanalyse* III (1913).

9. Letter from Edith Sitwell to John Lehmann, dated January 6, 1949 (reprinted in *Edith Sitwell: Selected Letters 1919-1964* (New York: The Vanguard Press, 1970), 164.

10. Helen Roeder, in her memoir "Ariel in the Tree Trunk," recalls lending a volume of Lawrence's stories to Welch in the early 1930's and his not returning it until the day he died in 1948. We cannot calculate the total effect Lawrence had upon Welch's writing, though Miss Roeder concludes, "Never was a borrowed book stolen with more profit."

11. The character Jim is based quite literally on Tom the woodman, whom Welch met and was impressed with sufficiently to describe at length in the *Journals* (p. 91 and 154).

Chapter Five

1. Dante, *The Divine Comedy*. The Inferno. Tr. by Louis Biancolli (New York: 1966), p. 1.

2. John Updike, "Promising," *The New Yorker* (Oct. 29, 1966), 236.

3. Defined by Charles Neider in his *Short Novels of the Masters* (New York, 1961), 23.

4. All page references are to the first American edition as published by the Humanities Research Center, The University of Texas (Austin, 1966).

5. Ruby Cohn, "A Few Novel Techniques of Denton Welch," *Perspective*, X, 3 (Summer-Autumn 1958), 157.

6. See Steffen Arndes Lübeck, *Hortus Sanitatis* (1492).

7. See G. S. Fraser, *The Modern Writer and His World* (New York, 1950), p. 134; and Edmund Wilson, "Maiden Voyage," *The New Yorker*, XXI (April 21, 1945), 83-84.

8. Francis Wyndham, "Twenty-five Years of the Novel," *The Craft of Letters in England*, ed. John Lehmann (Boston: 1957), p. 54.

9. Updike, *op. cit.*, 241.

10. Max Whittington-Egan, "On a Recaptured Joy," *Books and Bookmen*, XI, 9 (June, 1966), 40.

Chapter Six

1. As quoted by Welch in a letter to Maurice Cranston, dated September 19, 1942.

2. *A Last Sheaf* (London, 1951), p. 14.

3. The prototype for the fictional "Evergreen Seaton-Leverett" was possibly, with a change of sex, the real Prince Belosselsky, whom Welch observed and later visited. See the *Journals*, pp. 93-94.

4. The story was written on direct assignment from *Vogue*, which perhaps explains why it is so uninspired. See *Journals*, p. 133.

5. See Oliver, "Introduction," *A Last Sheaf*, pp. 7-8.

6. The character of the prisoner is most certainly a composite based on both the German prisoner Welch encountered on August 1, 1946, and also Harry Diedz, another prisoner with whom he shared Christmas dinner in that same year. See the *Journals*, pp. 219, 232.

7. Welch misquotes. Joyce Cary's actual phrase was, "it looks like a chamber pot crudely daubed with raspberry jam." This was the uncle's reply to Ann's question, "My face, uncle—isn't it all right?" Ann was addicted to using too much makeup. The exchange occurs in Chapter 7 of Cary's *To Be a Pilgrim*, which obviously impressed Welch.

8. Maurice Cranston, "Denton Welch," in *English Critical Essays*. Twentieth Century, Second Series. Selected and with an Introduction by Derek Hudson. London, 1958. p. 338.

Chapter Seven

1. For bibliographical details, see the overleaf to the volume as privately printed for James Campbell by the Lion and Unicorn Press. All textual references are to this 1958 edition.

2. Letter from Welch dated May 24, 1945, and presently in the archives of Routledge & Kegan Paul Ltd. Quoted by permission of Brian Southam, director.

3. Walter Allen, *The Modern Novel in Britain and the United States* (New York, 1964), p. 268.

4. John Bunyon, *Pilgrim's Progress*, The Harvard Classics Edition, ed. Charles W. Eliot (New York, 1937), p. 13.

5. *A Last Sheaf*, pp. 135-36.

6. "Gerald" clearly is the same individual Welch named "Mark Lynch" in *A Voice Through a Cloud*. Chapter Ten in that novel repeats some of the same material used in the shorter novel.

Chapter Eight

1. Quoted by Maurice Cranston in "Denton Welch," *The Spectator*, June 1, 1951.

2. Letter from Denton Welch to Henry Treece, dated May 14, 1943.

3. Letter from Denton Welch to Henry Treece, dated June 9, 1943.

4. Jocelyn Brooke, "Introduction," *The Denton Welch Journals*, p. xiv.

5. *Journals*, p. 84.

6. *Journals*, pp. 122-23.

7. All lines quoted are from those poems published in *A Last Sheaf*, pp. 211-40. There are other poems in manuscript among the Denton Welch papers at the University of Texas Library, but they are inferior in quality to those already published, as are those found scattered throughout the *Journals*.

8. John Carter, ed., *The Collected Poems of A. E. Housman* (New York, 1965), p. 80.

9. Maurice Cranston, *The Spectator*, June 1, 1951.

10. Letter from Rose Macaulay to Denton Welch, written in February, 1947 and quoted in the *Journals*, p. 237.

11. Cyril Connolly, *Previous Convictions* (London, 1963), p. 328.

12. "Introduction," *The Denton Welch Journals*, ed. Jocelyn Brooke (London, 1952), p. xiv.

13. See Neville Braybrooke, "Savage Wars," *The Quest*, I, 4 (Fall-Winter 1966), 66-76; and Gavin Lambert, "Confessions of a Charmer," *New York Times Book Review*, July 10, 1966, p. 46.

14. An insight echoed in substance nearly three decades later in Paul Simon and Arthur Garfunkel's popular recording, *The Sounds of Silence:* "The words of the prophets / are written on subway walls / and tenement halls. . . ."

15. John Lehmann, *I Am My Brother* (New York: 1960), p. 241.

16. W. H. Auden has written an account of this psychological condition as applied to J. R. Ackerley in particular and English homosexual writers in general in his "Papa Was a Wise Old Sly-Boots," *New York Review of Books,* March 27, 1969, pp. 3-4. Reprinted in his *Forwords and Afterwords,* (New York, 1973).

Chapter Nine

1. Letter from Edith Sitwell to John Lehmann, dated January 6, 1949. Reprinted in Edith Sitwell: *Selected Letters, 1919-1964.* Selected by John Lehmann and Derek Parker (New York, 1970), p. 164.

2. See the review by Peter Quinn, *Chicago Sun Book Week,* III, 39 (April 21, 1946), p. 8.

3. Updike, "Promising," *The New Yorker* (Oct. 29, 1966), p. 236.

4. Lehmann, *I Am My Brother* (New York, 1960), p. 241.

5. Letter from Denton Welch to Henry Treece of January 8, 1944.

6. Cohn, "A Few Novel Techniques of Denton Welch," *Perspective,* X, 3, (Summer-Autumn, 1958), 153-58.

7. Cranston, "Denton Welch," in *English Critical Essays,* Twentieth Century, Second Series. Ed. Derek Hudson (London, 1958), 333.

8. Auden, "Mr. Welch," *N.Y. Times Book Review* (March 18, 1945), p. 4.

9. Cranston, *English Critical Essays, loc cit.*

10. Walter Allen, *Tradition and Dream* (London, 1964), p. 288.

11. Pryce-Jones, *The Craft of Letters in England* (London, 1956), p. 36.

12. *Ibid.*

13. Quinn, *op. cit.*

14. Connolly, *Previous Convictions* (London, 1963), p. 329.

15. Anais Nin, *The Novel of the Future* (New York, 1968), 94.

16. Cohn, *Perspective,* X, 3 (Summer-Autumn 1958), p. 159.

17. Jean-Paul Sartre, "What Is Writing?", in *The Philosophy of Existentialism* (New York, 1965), 305.

18. Marcel Proust, quoted by Leon Edel in *The Modern Psychological Novel* (New York, 1961), p. 122.

Selected Bibliography

PRIMARY SOURCES
(Listed in chronological order)

Maiden Voyage. London: Routledge, 1943.
In Youth Is Pleasure. London: Routledge, 1945.
Brave and Cruel. London: Hamish Hamilton, 1948.
A Voice Through a Cloud. London: John Lehmann Ltd., 1950.
A Last Sheaf. London: John Lehmann Ltd., 1951.
The Denton Welch Journals. Edited and with an Introduction by Jocelyn Brooke. London: Hamish Hamilton, 1952.
I Left My Grandfather's House. London: Lion & Unicorn Press, 1958.
Denton Welch. A Selection from His Published Works. Edited and with an Introduction by Jocelyn Brooke. London: Chapman & Hall, 1963.

SECONDARY SOURCES

ADENEY, NOEL. *No Coward Soul* (London: The Hogarth Press, 1956). Thinly disguised biographical novel in which the hero is named "Merton" rather than Denton. Intimate view of Welch's life, ambitions, and limitations.
ALLEN, WALTER. *The Modern Novel in Britain and the United States* (New York: E. P. Dutton & Co., 1964), 268. Brief discussion of Welch's novels as "psychological casebooks rather than as fiction."
————. *Tradition and Dream. A Critical Survey of British and American Fiction from the 1920's to the Present Day* (Harmondsworth: Pelican Books), 1965. Same comments as the above.
ANON. "A Dream of Black Daimlers," *Times Literary Supplement,* No. 3,734 (Sept. 28, 1973), 1131-1132. Disability, genius, and "Romantic Agony" in Welch's work.

————. "A Rebel Youth," *Times Literary Supplement* XLII (Aug. 28, 1943), 3. English review of *Maiden Voyage* interprets that book's theme as "the self-centeredness of the lonely."

————. "Smooth Diamond," *Times Literary Supplement*, CXCVII, 3 (June 7, 1963), 407. Sees an analogical relation to the rustic poets of World War I; finds a poverty of understanding or sympathy with others in Welch's writing, probably due to his incapacity before experiencing any important emotional experiences.

————. "Minor Masterpiece," *Time*, LXXXVIII, 5 (July 29, 1966), 74. Review of the first American edition of *A Voice Through a Cloud:* "Echoing his own tragedy, it is a lyric, rebellious plaint of pain, fear and despair. . . . From his sickbed, Denton Welch saw life with the poignant clarity of a man seeing it for the last time."

————. *Choice*, IV, 7 (Sept. 1967). Review of first American edition of *A Voice Through a Cloud*.

ATHEY, ISABELLA. "A Boy's Life," *The Nation*, CLX (April 24, 1945), 462-64. An appreciation of *Maiden Voyage* as a novel about adolescence which does not fall into the clichés of such novels.

AUDEN, W. H. "Mr. Welch," *New York Times Book Review*, March 18, 1945, p. 4. Interesting if wrong-headed essay in which Auden sees Welch's "combination of scientific objectivity with subjective terror" combining to make his writing a "revealing comment on our historical situation."

BARRY, IRIS. "Young, Gifted and Unhappy," *New York Herald Tribune Weekly Book Review*, XXI, 32 (April 1, 1945), 10. Examines the physical and spiritual "embarrassments" in Welch's first book.

BASSO, HAMILTON. "Bread," *The New Yorker*, XXII (April 6, 1946), 106-08. Detailed review of *In Youth Is Pleasure* in which Basso accuses Welch of writing "blown-glass imitations of Baudelaire's flowers of evil."

BOLITHO, HECTOR. "In Welch Is Youth," *Town and Country*, C, 4284 (May, 1946), 150. Important personal interview with Welch, giving a portrait of the writer's temperament and working conditions.

————. "My Friendship with Denton Welch," *Texas Quarterly*, X, 4 (Winter, 1967), 235-40. New version of the above; some additional details and a photograph.

BRAYBROOKE, NEVILLE. "Savage Wars: A Study of the Journals of W. N. P. Barbellion and Denton Welch," *The Quest*, I, 4

(Fall-Winter 1966), 66-76. Comparison of the themes and methods of the two writers.

BROOKE, JOCELYN. "Introduction." *The Denton Welch Journals.* London: Hamish Hamilton, 1952. Critical appreciation; useful entrance to Welch's work.

――――. "Introduction." *Denton Welch. Extracts from His Published Works* London: Chapman & Hall, 1963. With the above, the two most useful sources of critical and biographical information to date.

――――. "The Dual Role: A Study of Denton Welch as Painter and Writer," *Texas Quarterly,* VI, 3 (Autumn, 1964), 120-27. Valuable exercise in comparison between Welch's accomplishments on the canvas and on the printed page. Considers the paintings to be strained and under-accomplished; the writing free and masterful: "In his pictures he is concerned with an artificial, an 'indoor' world of private symbols and obsessions; in his writing, he celebrates life itself . . . an 'outdoor' world in which nature, for the most part, predominates over art."

BUCKLE, RICHARD. "Denton Welch: a Few Quotes and a Biography," *Books and Bookmen,* XVIII, II (Aug., 1973), 32-34. Valuable chronology assembled independently of the one in this volume.

COHN, RUBY. "A Few Novel Techniques of Denton Welch," *Perspective,* X (Summer-Autumn 1958), 153-59. Illuminating analysis of Welch's imagery; a convincing demonstration of the centrality of the theme of "voyages" to his work.

CONNOLLY, CYRIL. *Previous Convictions.* London: Hamish Hamilton, 1963. Brief presentation of Welch's subject and style; discussion of the challenges involved in any writing of a journal.

COVENEY, PETER. *The Image of Childhood.* Revised Edition. Introduction by F. R. Leavis. Baltimore: Penguin Books, 1967. Welch briefly discussed as an example of a writer of post-Freudian persuasion whose central interest lay in the child.

CRANSTON, MAURICE W. "The Courage of Naîvite," *The Listener,* LXIX, 1783 (May 30, 1963), 922. Critical and biographical notes. Debunks several of Jocelyn Brooke's published assessments of Welch's character and achievement. Ultimately sees Welch as a strange and unclassifiable writer, like Cocteau.

――――. "Denton Welch." *Spectator Harvest.* Foreword by Wilson Harris. London: British Book Center, 1953 Originally published in *The Nineteenth Century and After,* CXLVIII, 884

(Oct., 1950), 237-45. Vital biographical memoir by one of Welch's close friends.

———. "Denton Welch," *Spectator*, June 1, 1951. Reprinted in *English Critical Essays*, Twentieth Century, Second Series. Selected and with an Introduction by Derek Hudson. London: Oxford University Press, 1958. Welch as a "novelist" in the Proustian sense; surveys a small part of his life with natural sharp insight.

DAVENPORT, BASIL. "What Will Become of Orvil Pym?", *Saturday Review*, XXIX (June 22, 1946), 24. Interesting discussion of *In Youth Is Pleasure* and the short story, "When I was Thirteen."

FERGUSON, HOWARD. *Discovery: Five Songs for Voice and Piano*. Words by Denton Welch. London: Boosey & Co., 1952. First musical setting of some of the verses from *A Last Sheaf*.

FRASER, G. S. *The Modern Writer and His World*. New York: Criterion, 1950. Early brief assessment; points out the author's limitations. Fraser sees Welch's work as an evasion of total problems, treating selected aspects of life rather than life as a whole. Compares Welch's work to that of William Sansom.

GRANSDEN, K. W. "Denton Welch's *Maiden Voyage*," *British Museum Quarterly*, XXI, 2 (July, 1957), 31-32. Biographical and bibliographical piece, on the occasion of the presentation of the manuscript of *Maiden Voyage* (in nine exercise books) to the Department of Manuscripts, The British Museum, by donor Sir Eric Miller. Attempts some bibliographical sleuthing among earlier drafts of the novel as well as in the abandoned novel which preceded it.

JOAD, C. E. M. *Decadence: A Philosophical Inquiry*. London: Faber & Faber, Ltd., 1948. Calls Welch's "Narcissus Bay" representative of decadent fiction; that is, works written under the assumption "that any experience is significant and worthy of record, irrespective of the quality of the experience or the nature of the 'object' of which it is an experience."

KARL, FREDERICK R. *The Contemporary English Novel*. New York: Farrar, Straus & Cudahy, 1962. Briefly notes that Welch's novels are concerned with "maturation" and attempts to interpret them in a homosexual light.

KUPFERBERG, HERBERT. "In Youth Is Pleasure," *New York Herald Tribune Weekly Book Review*, XXII, 34 (April 14, 1946), 14-16. Suggests the novel may be depicting the "decorous decadence" of a portion of English society just before World War II.

LEHMANN, JOHN. *A Nest of Tigers.* Boston: Atlantic-Little, Brown, 1968. Brief account of the significance Welch placed on his literary friendship with Dame Edith Sitwell.

———. *The Ample Proposition.* London: Eyre & Spottiswood, 1966, 103. Lehmann's role as publisher of Welch's last books; an appreciation of his talent.

———. *I Am My Brother.* New York: Reynal & Co., 1960. Critical and biographical comments. Lehmann agrees with Dame Edith Sitwell that Welch was "a born writer," but predicts that, had he lived, he would have developed into "the most disconcerting diarist of our day: an English Gide," because of his strict adherence to autobiographical subjects.

———. *In My Own Time.* Boston: Atlantic-Little, Brown, 1969. Reprinting of the same remarks above, but more accessible.

MAYNE, RICHARD. "Chinese Chippendale," *New Statesman,* LXV, 1679 (May 17, 1963), 751-52. Reassessment of Welch after twenty years; concludes he was "brave and defiant" to conceive those works during a period of total war. Feels Welch's alleged naivete was more knowing than most presume.

OLIVER, ERIC. "Foreword." *A Voice Through a Cloud.* London: John Lehmann, Ltd., 1950. Biographical remarks on Welch's health and his difficulty in completing this last novel by his closest friend and literary executor.

PEYRE, HENRI. *Literature and Sincerity.* New Haven and London: Yale University Press, 1963. Short commentary on Welch in relation to the genres of the confessional novel and the personal journal.

PHELPS, ROBERT and DEANE, PETER. *The Literary Life.* New York: Farrar, Straus & Giroux, 1968. Historical perspective for Welch's publications.

PHILLIPS, ROBERT. *"Brave and Cruel:* The Short Stories of Denton Welch," *Studies in Short Fiction,* VII, 3 (Summer 1970), 357-77. Extended critiques on all the stories in Welch's first and most important collection; alludes to remaining stories.

———. *"A Voice Through a Cloud:* Denton Welch's Ultimate Voyage," *The Centennial Review,* XV, 2 (Spring 1971), 218-28. Welch and the "literature of sickness," his last novel interpreted with relation to Schopenhauer's "Web of Maya." Reprinted with a few changes as Chapter Six of the present Twayne volume.

———. "Syracuse Has Important Denton Welch Manuscript," *Syracuse University Library Bulletin,* XIV (June 3, 1970), 3-4.

Traces the published and unpublished correspondence between Welch and Lester G. Wells (Rare Book Librarian and Curator of Manuscripts, Syracuse University) which began in 1945 and culminated in presentation of the manuscript, "When I Was Thirteen" to Syracuse. (See also *The Denton Welch Journals* for the author's account of this exchange.)

PRYCE-JONES, ALAN. "The Personal Story" *The Craft of Letters in England*. Ed. John Lehmann. London: The Cresset Press, 1956. Welch and the genre of the obliquely written autobiography.

RABINOVITZ, RUBIN. *The Reaction Against Experiment in the English Novel, 1950-1960*. New York: Columbia University Press, 1967. Quotes C. P. Snow's defense of Denton Welch as a highly talented writer who deserves wider readership today, and one belonging in the stream of Dorothy Richardson and James Joyce.

RICHARDSON, KENNETH, ed. *Twentieth Century Writing*. London: Newnes Books, 1969. 637-38. Welch in an historical view.

ROEDER, HELEN. "Ariel in the Tree Trunk." *I Left My Grandfather's House*. London: Lion & Unicorn Press, 1958. Personal impressions of Welch, particularly of his art school days, by one who knew him for a decade.

SNOW, C. P. *Times Literary Supplement*, Dec. 28, 1952, p. 7. Welch in relation to stream-of-consciousness novelists.

SITWELL, EDITH. "A Foreword." *Maiden Voyage*. London: Routledge, 1943. Concludes that "Mr. Welch may easily prove to be, not only a born writer, but a very considerable one."

———. *Taken Care Of*. New York: Atheneum, 1965. Brief biographical note concerning Welch's visit to Walter Sickert at Convent Garden; the basis for Welch's first published piece.

———. *Selected Letters, 1919-1964*. New York: The Vanguard Press, 1970. Important series of letters from Dame Edith to Welch, spanning September, 1942, until his death in December, 1948, in which his work and his life are treated with Sitwellian enthusiasm and sympathy.

SITWELL, OSBERT. *Noble Essences*. Boston: Atlantic-Little, Brown, 1950. Confirmation of the Sickert-Welch-Edith Sitwell chronology.

SMITH, JANET ADAM. "Growing Up," *The Spectator*, CLXX, 5994 (May 14, 1943), 456-58. Consideration of *Maiden Voyage*.

STERN, JAMES. "The Artist as a Young Man," *The New Republic*, CXII, 12 (March 19, 1945), 393. Appreciative review of Welch's first published novel.

————. "An Orvil Bore," *The New Republic*, CXIV, 13 (April 1, 1946), 452-54. Attack on *In Youth Is Pleasure;* contains an interesting interpretation of its "blood imagery."

SWINNERTON, FRANK. *Figures in the Foreground.* New York: Doubleday, 1964. Personal anecdote about correspondence with Welch. Account of Welch's supposed "writer's block" after completing *Maiden Voyage.*

SYMONS, JULIAN. *The Spectator*, 235 (May 31, 1963), 709. Sympathetic review of Jocelyn Brooke's selection from Welch's published books.

THOORENS, LEON. "Denton Welch ou le Defi au Néant," *Revue Generale Belge* (Brussels) (December, 1956), 339-42. Analysis of Welch as a nihilist.

TINDALL, WILLIAM YORK. *Forces in Modern British Literature, 1185-1946.* New York: Alfred A. Knopf, 1949. Compares Welch's novels favorably with Thomas Wolfe's *Look Homeward, Angel* and Dylan Thomas's *Portrait of the Artist as a Young Dog.*

TOYNBEE, PHILIP. "Repton to China," *The New Statesman and Nation*, XXV (June 12, 1943), 390. *Maiden Voyage* as autobiography.

TRILLING, DIANA. *The Nation*, CLXII (April 6, 1946), 406. Review of Welch's second novel.

UPDIKE, JOHN. "Promising," *The New Yorker* (Oct. 29, 1966), 236-41. Valuable discussion of *A Voice Through a Cloud* as an existential and prophetic document, "a proclamation of our terrible fragility," as well as a definition of both circumstantial and gnostic suspense in fiction such as Welch's.

WALDHORN, ARTHUR and HILDA. *Rite of Becoming: Stories and Studies of Adolescence.* New York: World Publishing Co., 1966. Psychoanalytical explication of the story "When I was Thirteen."

WEST, PAUL. *The Modern Novel.* I. London: Hutchinson & Co., 1963. Welch and the modern movement; comparison with Capote and Isherwood.

WHITTINGTON-EGAN, M. "On a Recaptured Joy," *Books & Bookmen*, XI, 9 (June, 1966), 40. Appreciation of *A Voice Through a Cloud.*

WILSON, EDMUND. "Blushes and Shudders," *The New Yorker*, XXI (April 21, 1945), 83-84. Style and vision in Welch's first book.

WYKES-JOYCE, MAX. *Triad of Genius.* London: Peter Owen, Ltd., 1953. Welch's visual sense briefly compared with that of Gerard Manley Hopkins.

WYNDHAM, FRANCIS. "Twenty-five Years of the Novel." *The Craft of Letters in England.* Ed. John Lehmann. London: The Cresset Press, 1956. Discussion of Welch with other English novelists writing after 1940 who wrote "independent of any literary tradition."

YOUNG, MARGUERITE. "Schoolboy," *New York Times Book Review,* March 31, 1946, 6. Useful discussion of Welch's method and imagination; centers around *In Youth Is Pleasure.*

Index

Index